INSIGHT

SINGAPORE

'STONYCROFT'
18 QUARRY LANE
WINTERBOURNE DOWN
BS36 1DB
Tel. (01454) 773691

Discovery
CHANNEL

APA PUBLICATIONS

Part of the Langenscheidt Publishing Group

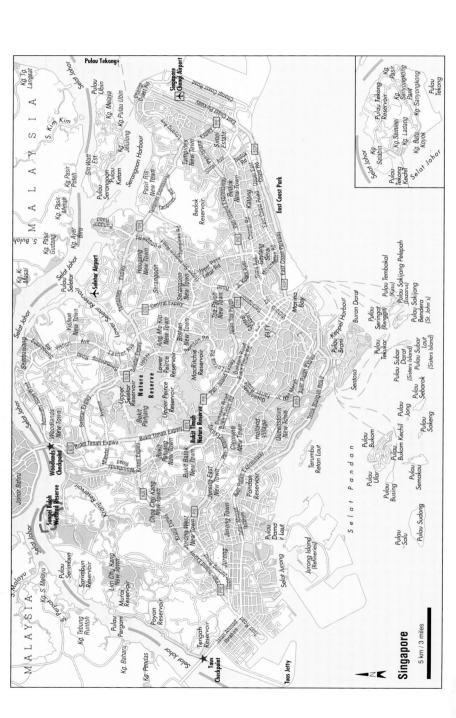

Singapore

5 km / 3 miles

Welcome

This is one of 133 itinerary-based Pocket Guides produced by the editors of Insight Guides, whose books have set the standard for visual travel guides since 1970. With top-quality photography and authoritative recommendations, this guidebook brings you the very best of Singapore in a series of 15 tours devised by Insight's Singapore correspondent, Tisa Ng.

The island city of Singapore is renowned not only as a melting pot of Asian cultures and a great destination for a shopping spree, but also as one of the culinary centres of Asia. Modernity and tradition go hand in hand in this amazing city-state, so expect to see Muslim mosques and Chinese and Hindu temples huddling incongruously between towering skyscrapers and luxury hotels. Asian and Western culture and values meet and mingle in this cosmopolitan city, giving rise to eclectic lifestyles, heavenly cuisines and a funky, but still wholesome, nightlife scene. All of Singapore's must-see sights are covered in the first three full-day itineraries while the remaining options are covered in the following 10 tours. For those with time to spare, there are rewarding daytrips to offshore isles and longer overnight excursions to places in neighbouring Malaysia and Indonesia. Chapters on shopping, eating out and nightlife, plus a useful practical information section on travel essentials complete this reader-friendly guide.

Tisa Ng was born in China, grew up in Hong Kong, completed her education in France and Britain, and now calls Singapore home. Her truly cosmopolitan background is perfect for capturing the eclectic flavour of Singapore. Even though she has lived here for many years, Singapore never fails to surprise Tisa – and she is continually discovering new and fascinating nooks which hide between the glass and steel structures of the city centre and in its charmingethnic enclaves and suburbs. She has worked in both the print media as well as television and radio in addition to a varied career in arts management. She currently runs her own events management company.

This new edition was completely restructured and rewritten by Tisa and owes its foundations to the original edition put together by Marianne Rankin.

History and Culture

From the founding of Singapore by Stamford Raffles to its rise as a modern business hub, this is an introduction to the forces that have shaped this vibrant city **11**

City Itineraries

Pages 2/3: the ever-changing Singapore skyline
Pages 8/9: Chinatown calligrapher at work

History & Culture

Singapore is a small city in a big hurry, always striving for success and rushing to be number one in everything that it does. Given its outstanding economic success since independence in 1965, there is unrelenting pressure to perform and maintain its strong economic position. One possible reason for this apparent anxiety is its small size. Singapore is a tiny island-state of about 699 sq km (267 sq miles). Together with 58 smaller islands, it occupies less land than the area covered under the red dot on which it is represented on most world maps.

It has a population of over 4.3 million, with the optimal number targeted at 5.5 million, despite pressures on land and other natural resources. However, achieving the desired increase is proving to be a challenge for the government, as Singapore suffers from the common developed country phenomenon of declining birth rates. Coupled with a greying population, this has become an issue of serious concern. In 2004, the government enhanced the 'Baby Bonus' package, initially introduced in the year 2000, as an incentive for Singaporeans to marry and to reproduce.

These limitations notwithstanding, Singapore shows no sign of allowing its destiny to be limited by size, and actively engages the rest of the world, often punching above its weight in international affairs. It has taken on an increasing important regional and international role through participation in organisations like the UN and the Association of Southeast Asian Nations (Asean).

Connecting with the World

The awareness of the need to connect beyond its limited shores can be seen in the priority given to developing a world-class port, an award-winning airport, a national airline that is a serious international player and in gearing Singapore up for the borderless new economy. Working with multi-national corporations and laying out the red carpet for foreign talent continue to underpin nation-building policies, occasionally giving rise to rumblings from locals who sometimes feel under-appreciated.

Even in the development of local arts and culture, in urban conservation and management of physical heritage, the needs and expectations of a transient population have been high on the agenda, with the Singapore Tourism Board playing a significant role.

So, as a visitor to Singapore, you are a very welcome guest; and if some of the people you meet seem less than gracious despite the national courtesy campaigns, it is often because they are in a hurry, and are under constant pressure to upgrade, update and improve themselves. Time is perhaps the greatest luxury in the rush for a better future.

Left: Fort Canning viewed from the sea in the 1900s
Right: Merlion, symbol of Singapore

Money Matters

Also, do not be fazed by questions about money. No rudeness or intrusiveness is intended. A survey in the leading local newspaper in 2000 showed that money was the primary concern of over 50 percent of Singaporeans. It is almost customary at house-warming parties to entertain questions about the cost of the flat or house, mortgage deals and renovation bills. Often this will be related immediately to the hosts' income and net worth. A compliment about a watch or a piece of jewellery will often be followed by questions about its price and where it was purchased. Or the taxi driver will remark that it cost a great deal of money to fly all the way from your hometown.

If you can report a really good deal, you will be sincerely admired for it, so don't be shy with the information. If you feel uncomfortable about revealing personal information, give a general range representative of market prices in your country instead. Think of it as cultural exchange.

Early History and the Founding of Singapore

Perhaps the most impressive deal in Singapore's history is the one that Sir Stamford Raffles closed with Sultan Hussein of Johor in 1819. As Lieutenant-Governor of Bencoolen, Raffles was tasked to set up a trading post for the East India Company. He achieved this by means of a treaty with Sultan Hussein to lease Singapore at 5,000 Spanish dollars per year, with another annuity of 3,000 dollars for his local resident, the Temenggong.

Singapore was something of a sleepy island at the time, home to the Orang Laut or Sea People, with a reputation for being a haunt of pirates in the area. So property prices were understandably low: it had already seen better times in its short history.

In the 3rd century, there is a Chinese reference to P'u Luo Chung or 'Island at the end of the Peninsula', which historians think might be Singapore. In the 13th century, Marco Polo mentions a large and noble city, Chiamassie, on the route to Sumatra; and according to the *Sejarah Melayu* or Malay Annals, Temasek or 'Sea Town' was a thriving port in the 14th cen-

tury. It was subsequently renamed Lion City or Singapura by a visiting prince of the Sri Vijayan empire, Sang Nila Utama, who sighted an unusual beast that resembled a lion. Towards the end of the 14th century, the island fell victim to the conflicting expansionist ambitions of the Ayutthaya (Siam) and Majapahit (Java) empires, and slid into decline.

Stamford Raffles, accorded the title 'founder of Singapore', referred to it correctly as an ancient city before ever stepping foot on its shores, and wrote of its 'classic grounds ... the lines of the old city, and of its defences ... still to be traced' during his first visit in 1819.

Left: a 17th-century map of the Malay peninsula

Upon securing the lease, Raffles began to develop the settlement and despite his frequent absences, when Resident Colonel Farquhar was in charge, he was ultimately responsible for the layout of the city. He determined the location of the government sector, the European town, and areas for the Bugis, Arab, Chulia and Malay communities. Chinatown was organised so that the Chinese from different provinces lived in their own sections within the area to the southwest of the Singapore River. Construction of masonry houses with tiled roofs was also prescribed by Raffles, as were the 'five-footways' or covered pavements in front of all houses in the ethnic quarters.

Indians were among the first migrants to Singapore; Naraina Pillai from Penang being possibly the very first. Large numbers of Chinese, mainly from Malacca, swelled the population from 1,000 to 5,000 in the first six months of 1819 alone. Trade flourished and the settlement grew in prosperity, attracting further waves of economic migrants. The British took full control of the island in 1824, with John Crawford as the second Resident. It was by then home to 11,000 people, mostly Malays and Bugis, with smaller numbers of Indians, Europeans, Armenians and Arabs. The Chinese, already a significant proportion of the population, would increase to 28,000 by 1849.

In 1826, Singapore became part of the Straits Settlements with Penang and Malacca. Trading opportunities and prosperity grew in the region with the decline of the China trade monopoly held by the East India Company, and when restrictions imposed by the Dutch were lifted.

In 1867, the Straits Settlements became a Crown Colony and Singapore's position as a port and coaling station on the trade route between Europe and East Asia further increased with the opening of the Suez Canal in 1869.

Immigrant Populations

This economic success was borne on the backs of immigrant labour, including Indian convict labourers who started arriving in 1825, and built much of the early infrastructure. A large proportion of the early immigrants had no intention of making Singapore a permanent home. Apart from the distinctive Samsui women from south China, who foreswore marriage and worked on construction sites heaving baskets of building material slung on a pole over their shoulders, most of the immigrants were men. In 1836, there were 14,642 Chinese males to every 1,000 Chinese females, and 9,580 Indian males to every 1,000 Indian females.

With the focus solely on sending money home or saving up for an eventual triumphant return, very basic living conditions were endured with

Above: Sir Stamford Raffles, Singapore's founder

stoicism, or with opium as an escape. Sanitation was primitive and the mortality rate was as high as 40 per 1,000 at the end of the 19th century.

Unsanitary 'Asiatic habits' were held at least partly accountable for the deplorable state of affairs, and it was not until 1878 that the first municipal waterworks was opened. Chinese merchant and philanthropist Tan Kim Seng financed the project in 1857, stipulating that the water should be free for the whole population.

Self-help and community support were important aspects of immigrant life. Among the Chinese, clan associations led by successful businessmen in the community formed a parallel system of welfare and justice, filling vacuums left by the colonial government, by giving aid and resolving disputes. Each of the three main dialect groups, the Hokkiens, Cantonese and Teochews, had its own association by the 1820s.

The number of Malays also increased, although not at the same rate as the Chinese. Because of the scarcity of Chinese women, Chinese men married local Malay women, giving rise to the Straits Chinese or Peranakan culture. The *baba* (men) and *nyonya* (women) adopted much of the Malay culture, including food, fashion and a distinctive Singapore-Malay patois.

In the Indian community, divisions of caste, ethnic and sub-ethnic groupings, as well as place of origin extended to immigrant family networks. South Indian Hindus formed the majority, but there were also significant numbers of South Indian Muslims and North Indian Sindhis and Gujeratis.

Japanese Occupation

The hardships endured by early immigrants pale in comparison to the three years under Japanese rule from February 1942 to September 1945, when the island was renamed again, this time as Syonan, 'Light of the South'.

Britain's 'Fortress Singapore', armed and impregnable against any attack from the sea, was brilliantly taken by Tomoyuki Yamashita, the 'Tiger of Malaya', with a surprise overland attack from the north. The British forces surrendered within a week after suffering appalling losses.

Allied prisoners of war were incarcerated in camps like Changi, sent to North Borneo, or to work on the notorious Burma railway. All Chinese males between 18 and 50 had to register with the Japanese forces, and any undesirable element was purged. The *Kempeitai* meted out brutal treatment for any infringement, including a failure to bow appropriately, and many local women were forced into prostitution as 'comfort women'. Today, older Singaporeans who came through the period relatively unscathed can still recall vividly the constant fear, hunger and deprivation.

Above: a Straits Chinese or Peranakan family of Chinese and Malay heritage
Right: Lee Kuan Yew leads PAP's victory march, 1959

Independence and Nation Building

After the Japanese surrender in 1945, the British returned and, for several years, attempted to retain their former hold on the colony. But times and attitudes had changed, independence was in the air, and after attempts at compromise by the British against a background of insurrection led by the Communist Party of Malaya, Singapore attained self-government on 5 June 1959. Lee Kuan Yew was sworn in as Prime Minister of an independent Singapore, having led his People's Action Party (PAP) to victory in the first General Election.

Merger with Malaya in the Federation of Malaysia took place in September 1963, to the displeasure of neighbouring Indonesia, which then began three years of armed confrontation with the Federation. But racial tension and political differences soon led to a split with Malaysia, and on 9 August 1965, Singapore was removed from the Federation of Malaysia to become an independent nation.

Prospects looked grim for Singapore. Basic needs required urgent attention. The Housing Development Board (HDB) was established to provide homes for the people of Singapore. In the first phase, the priority was speed. By 1990, the HDB had built over 600,000 apartments. Thereafter, building continued but at a slower pace. With increasing affluence, the early functional accommodation no longer satisfied expectations, and an extensive national programme of upgrading existing flats was started by the ruling party. In order to give every citizen a stake in what has come to be known as Singapore Inc, home ownership was encouraged through direct subsidies and tax breaks. Some 92 percent home ownership was recorded in the 2000 census. In 2005, it was estimated that 83 percent of the resident population live in HDB-built flats.

In terms of improvements to basic living conditions, post-independence achievements are hard to dispute. Infant mortality, which was 82 per 1,000 in 1950, fell to 2 per 1,000 in 2004. The 'economic miracle' – spurred by foreign investment and shrewd economic planning – which saw Singapore achieve a GNP per capita income that was the highest in Asia after Japan by the 1980s, and outstrip Britain in the 1990s, was sustained beyond the Asian economic crisis which hit the region towards the end of that decade.

In 1990, Prime Minister Lee Kuan Yew handed over leadership of the PAP to Goh Chok Tong. In 2000, the government announced a growth rate of over 10 percent for that year, thanks to enlightened policies and good management. But this recovery did not sustain. Rising costs and wages coupled with competition from China and India continued to hamper growth. The economy was further dented in 2003 by the Severe Acute Respiratory Syndrome (SARS) outbreak, with unemployment hitting an unprecedented 5.5 percent. Thankfully, the situation has improved – in 2005, the economy grew by an encouraging 6.4 percent.

Although a multi-party system exists in Parliament, the ruling PAP party has not been seriously challenged and has been returned to power at everY election since 1959. In order to reflect non-partisan views, nominated Members of Parliament (NMPs) were introduced in 1991. The ruling party's unwritten contract with its voters is to provide a high standard of living. It is a contract on which the political leadership has generally delivered, and they are well paid for it, not only in terms of retaining power, but also in remuneration. At roughly S$1.7m (US$1m) per annum, the Prime Minister's salary is significantly higher than that of his counterparts in Britain, Canada and the US. In 2004, the PAP's stranglehold on power was set in place when Lee Hsien Loong – son of former PM Lee Kuan Yew – took over as Prime Minister.

Not Thoroughly Modern

Visitors to Singapore are often either impressed or dismayed to find a modern city with gleaming tower blocks somewhat lacking in exotic mystery, and a dignified five-star deluxe Raffles Hotel with no trace of the dowdy *grande dame* in faded glory. But clean water, a safe environment and communications that you can count on are generally appreciated by all.

And despite all the outward appearances of a modern cosmopolitan city, Singapore remains Asian at heart. Confucian values are extolled, and the official view upholds the traditional family structure with the patriarch as head

of the household. Due deference is the expected norm for those in positions of authority, and 'connections' or *guanxi* is an acknowledged asset in business.

Increasingly, the government recognises the need for a creative and lateral thinking population to fuel the economic successes of the future. Although this has seen some relaxation of rules in the arts scene, social behaviour and in the political arena, everyone knows that there are prescribed boundaries. Whatever the measure, pragmatism has always been a guiding principle, and the main thrust of development is to make Singapore a great place to do business. It also happens to be a great place to share with locals their two favourite hobbies: shopping and eating.

Left: CBD area from Elgin Bridge

HISTORY HIGHLIGHTS

1819 Sir Stamford Raffles sets up a trading post for the British East India Company with the agreement of the Sultan of Johor and the Temenggong, his representative on the island.

1824 The Sultan cedes Singapore in perpetuity to the British.

1826 Singapore, with Malacca and Penang, becomes part of the Straits Settlements, under the control of British India.

1867 The Colonial Office in London takes over control of Singapore.

1942 The Japanese invade and occupy Singapore.

1945 The Japanese surrender and the Allied Forces return.

1946 Singapore becomes a Crown Colony.

1948 The British allow limited elections to the Legislative Council. A state of emergency is declared in June, following the Malayan Communist Party's uprising against British imperialism.

1951 Legislative Council election. Singapore is formally proclaimed a city with a royal charter.

1955 The Rendel Constitution granted by the British leads to elections; David Marshall becomes Chief Minister.

1956 Lim Yew Hock takes over as Chief Minister.

1958 A Constitutional Agreement for partial independence for Singapore is signed in London.

1959 The first general elections for a fully elected Legislative Assembly; People's Action Party's (PAP) Lee Kuan Yew becomes Prime Minister.

1963 Singapore becomes part of the Federation of Malaysia.

1965 Singapore, forced out of the Federation of Malaysia, becomes an independent sovereign nation.

1967 Singapore issues its own currency.

1968 In the general elections, PAP wins all 58 seats.

1981 In a by-election, Mr J B Jeyaratnam of the Workers' Party wins the first seat to be held by an opposition member.

1984 PAP loses two of 79 seats in the general elections.

1987 The US$5 billion Mass Rapid Transit (MRT) railway system opens.

1988 Under a revised constitution the PAP wins 80 seats in general elections, with the Singapore Democratic Party (SDP) winning one seat, and two members of the Workers' Party declared non-constituency Members of Parliament (MPs).

1990 Prime Minister Lee Kuan Yew hands leadership of PAP over to Goh Chok Tong, who forms the new government. Lee is appointed as Senior Minister.

1991 PAP wins the elections, but this time loses four seats to the opposition.

1993 Ong Teng Cheong is elected as President in Singapore's first presidential election.

1998 The Second Link, the new causeway to Malaysia, opens.

1999 S R Nathan from the minority Indian race is appointed President.

2001 PAP wins 75.3 percent of votes in general elections. Global economic downturn leads to a 4.7 percent unemployment rate, a 15-year high.

2002 The landmark Esplanade – Theatres on the Bay opens.

2003 Outbreak of Severe Acute Respiratory Syndrome (SARS) in April is brought under control, but the economy is dented. The North-East Line extension of the MRT opens.

2004 Lee Hsien Loong takes over as Prime Minister.

2006 PAP wins all but two seats in general elections, taking 66.6 percent of the votes.

history/culture

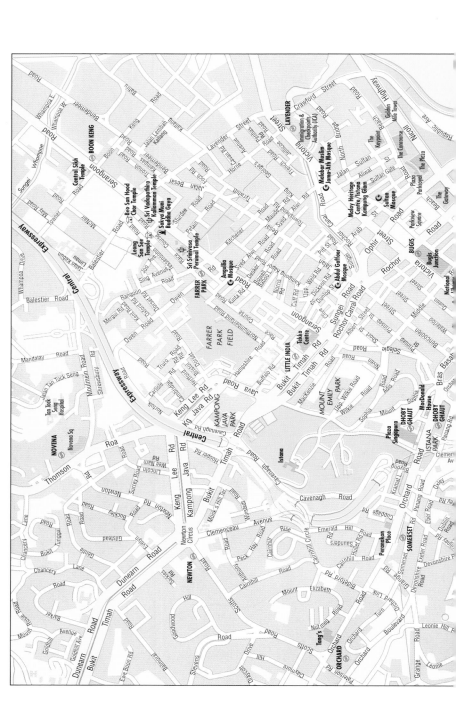

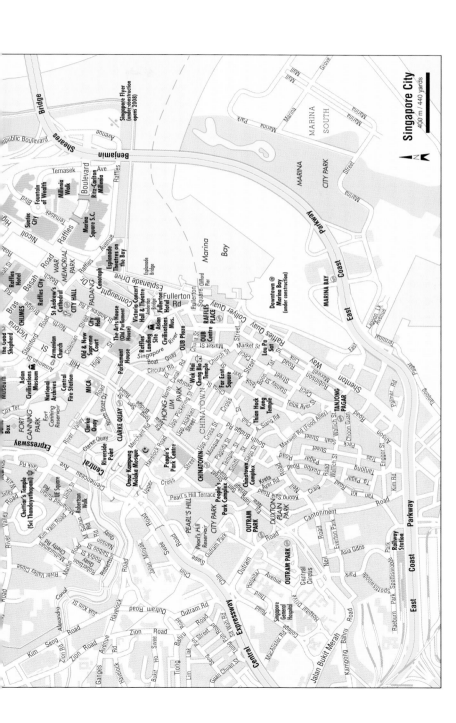

Singapore City

400 m / 440 yards

City Itineraries

The following tours introduce you to the amazing diversity contained in tiny Singapore, from gleaming towers and charming ethnic enclaves to primary rainforest and offshore islands. The full-day *Itineraries 1–3* are walking tours designed to get you acquainted with life in the city – where doing business is a priority. The first tour takes you through the Central Business District (CBD), where Singapore's status as a leading Asian financial centre is honed. The second tour of Orchard Road – considered by some to be one of the best shopping streets in the world – is a favourite for most tourists. *Itinerary 3* covers the Civic District, where government offices and impressive museums are housed in tastefully restored heritage buildings.

If you have more time, or would like to head straight to a special area of interest, take your pick from the remaining *Itineraries 4–13,* which suggest activities for different times of the day. Anticipate a good deal of walking, and since it is hot and humid most of the year, a good sunblock and cool, lightweight cotton clothes are recommended.

A Safe City

Singapore is one of the safest cities in the world; so, if you see a little alleyway that looks promising, go ahead and explore it. And while walking you will come across food options everywhere. That Singaporeans live to eat is an old joke, and witnessing the passion with which the locals tuck into their favourite dishes will give you a sense of what makes them tick. In addition to restaurants, most shopping centres have a food court. Coffee culture, too, is alive and kicking, from simple neighbourhood places to chains like Coffee Bean and Starbucks. Smoking is now banned in cafés and restaurants, but some eating places have permits enabling them to have outdoor sections for smokers.

Downtown Singapore is compact and easy to get around. Mass Rapid Transit (MRT) trains are a quick way to travel between most urban areas. Many of the starting points in the itineraries that follow are accessible by train. Air-conditioned buses are comfortable and a good way to see the sights, but you may have to wait a bit before a particular service arrives. The Singapore Trolley and SIA Hop-on bus, which offer unlimited rides, are other leisurely options. Taxis are inexpensive, air-conditioned and a good choice, especially for those destinations not well-served by buses or trains *(pages 91–3)*.

Singaporeans are a busy lot caught up in the business of making a living. While many are reserved about approaching strangers, they are not unfriendly. Don't be alarmed if you are seemingly addressed as family; 'auntie' and 'uncle' are informal, old-fashioned terms of address which apply to anyone older than yourself. Try this out, and make new friends.

Left: Palladian-style arched windows of a shophouse
Right: well-signposted street

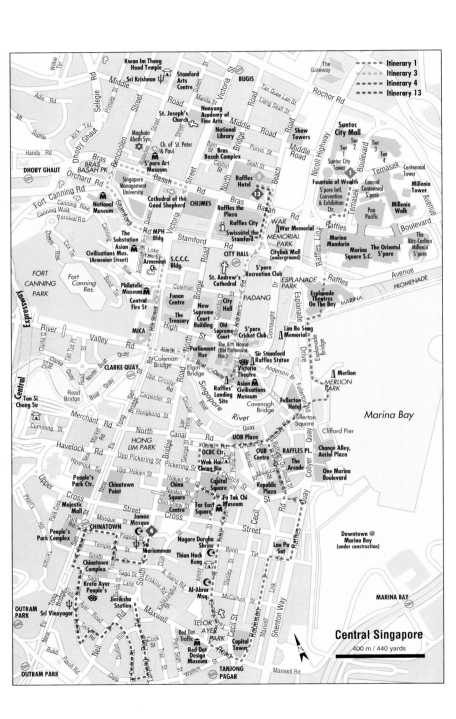

Central Singapore

400 m / 440 yards

Itinerary 1
Itinerary 3
Itinerary 4
Itinerary 13

Right: the Central Business District, Caltex House

1. Central Business District *(see map, p22)*

Explore the commercial heart of Singapore with this walk past the gleaming towers of the Central Business District and the sprawling developments of Marina Bay. Along the way, visit religious monuments established by early migrants for a taste of the island's old days as a port of call.

Take the train to Raffles Place MRT *Station or get a taxi to drop you off opposite Republic Plaza on D'almeida Street*

Since the conduct of business is crucial to Singapore's existence, start at **Raffles Place**, a prime address in the **Central Business District** (CBD) where major financial institutions surround a little green space: the dark mirrored façade of **Republic Plaza**, the sharp-edged **OUB Centre**, and the two towers of **UOB Plaza I** and **II** with an open atrium between them. All three buildings are 280m (920ft) tall, the maximum height allowed by the civil aviation authorities.

In the old days, Raffles Place was known as Commercial Square and it was here that Singapore's first department stores started life: John Little and Robinsons. The latter, founded in 1858, was an important lifestyle icon in upper-crust society, but in 1972, it was destroyed in a fire. Both stores are now located in Orchard Road *(see page 32)*. The design of the main entrance of the **Raffles Place** MRT **Station** recalls the glory days of Commercial Square.

At the riverside end of Raffles Place is a monumental sculpture entitled *Progress and Advancement,* by Yang Ying-Feng, which was commissioned and presented by banker-philanthropist Lien Ying Chow on the auspicious date of 8 August 1988. Eight is a homonym for prosperity in Chinese, and the sculpture is a celebration of the commercial life of the city. Across the road, at one side of the UOB Plaza atrium, Salvador Dali's *Homage to Newton* in bronze with dark patina stands. Turn left into **Chulia Street** and mingle with the office workers on their way to work. Many stop to pick up breakfast from the outlets fronting Market Street; business is brisk on most weekday mornings and many customers depart with their morning coffee suspended in transparent plastic bags.

Continue into **South Canal Road** to view an impressive reclining figure by Henry Moore, in front of the **OCBC Centre**. Unprepared for Singapore's humid climate, the bronze sculpture suffered from corrosion soon after instal-

lation, and was subsequently treated to acquire the golden hue it wears today. Almost opposite is **Boat Quay** *(see page 85)*, a lively waterfront area after dark for young Singaporeans and expats bent on partying all night long. The stretch of restaurants and pubs here occupy old shophouses that once served as warehouses for Chinese traders in the old days.

Chinese Charm

Past the Henry Moore figure, turn left into **Synagogue Street**, which takes you to Church Street. Turn left where at the corner with **Philip Street** you will find the Taoist **Wak Hai Cheng Bio Temple** (also called Yueh Hai Cheng). The temple was built in the 1850s by the Teochew community for the protection of traders travelling between Singapore and China – at the time Phillip Street, just round the corner, was close to the sea.

Cross **Church Street**, and turn right past **Capital Square** where a wall with sheets of water cascading invites prosperity; water has associations with wealth and also serves as a reminder of how close the coast used to be. Turn left though a gap in the building to **Far East Square**, a restaurant-office complex in which several of the restored buildings date from the 1820s.

If you haven't had breakfast, stop by **Ya Kun** (18 China Street) for mid-morning coffee and toast spread with *kaya*, a fragrant coconut custard. If not enter Far East Square by the **Metal Gate** – five gates mark entrances to the complex, each representing one of the elements that make up the Chinese universe: metal, wood, water, fire and earth. Turn left and exit by the **Water Gate**. Explore the area, then walk along what used to be Pekin Street (now a pedestrian walkway) to **Telok Ayer Street**. Just opposite is the mammoth **China Square Food Centre**. The **Teahouse** restaurant (tel: 6533 0660) on the third floor serves Chinese snacks called *dim sum* all day long.

Further down Telok Ayer Street is the **Fu Tak Chi Museum** (daily 10am–10pm; free; tel: 6532 7868) at No 76, where on display are artefacts and memorabilia from the area's earliest days.

Top: redeveloped Boat Quay is now home to some great eateries and bars
Above: signage – Far East Square

Mosques and Temples

Make your way along Telok Ayer Street, with its rows of pre-war shop-houses, many of which have been converted into offices. On the corner of Boon Tat and Telok Ayer streets is the **Nagore Durgha Shrine**, built in the late 1820s by Tamil Muslims as a meeting place and house of worship. Closed indefinitely for major renovations, the temple was known for its traditional pierced-work balustrade, Corinthian pillars and stepped towers.

Next is the richly ornamented **Thian Hock Keng Temple** (daily 7.30am–5.30pm), the oldest Chinese temple in Singapore. Early immigrants from southern China disembarking from crowded 'hell-ship' junks went straight to the temple to thank the Goddess Ma Zu Po for a safe journey. Inside, her statue, brought from Amoy, China, in 1840, still stands between the god of prosperity and the god of health. The temple was completed in 1842 by craftsmen using materials imported from China, and without the use of a single nail. Until 1887, when Telok Ayer Basin was filled, the temple stood at the waterfront.

A little further on the right at No 192 is the **Masjid Al Abrar**, built in the mid-1850s to replace the original thatched hut established on the site in 1827. Follow the curve of the road past the **Telok Ayer Chinese Methodist Church** on your left. Cut through Telok Ayer Park to the **red dot Traffic** building for a stopover at the **red dot design museum** (Fri–Tues 11am–8pm; admission fee; tel: 6534 7194). On show are slickly designed products from around the world that have won the prestigious red dot design award.

Turn left from the red dot Traffic building and walk along Maxwell Road before crossing Cecil Street to **Capital Tower**. Buy an iced latté from the Starbucks café on the ground floor and relax at the courtyard where a whimsical sculpture fountain called *Shimmering Pearls* takes centrestage. The multi-coloured baubles suspended on steel rods and floating above a pool of water is the work of local sculptor Han Sai Por.

Head back towards the centre of the CBD along **Robinson Road**. At the corner with Boon Tat Street, is **Lau Pa Sat** or 'Old Market', a Victorian cast-iron structure dating from 1894, which houses a food court and souvenir stalls. In the evenings, **Boon Tat Street** is closed to traffic and transformed into an alfresco dining area famous for *satay*.

Turn left and continue up **Raffles Quay** – just opposite massive construction is in progress for the new business and leisure hub Downtown@Marina Bay – to **Finlayson Green**, where you cut through Ocean Building to return to the Raffles Place MRT Station. Now is a good time for a break. For a cool respite from the hubbub, make your way past Maybank Tower to the luxurious **Fullerton Hotel** at 1 Fullerton Square. Opened in 2000, this hotel occupies a historic building named after Robert Fullerton, first governor of the Straits Settlements (1824–30). The building was erected in 1928 and housed the former General Post Office for many years. Now beautifully restored with its

Right: altar table, Thian Hock Keng Temple

original Palladian-style façade relatively intact, it has a contemporary interior filled with natural light from a central atrium created by punching out the old ceiling. The stylish **Town Restaurant** (tel: 6877 8128) has a nice selection of food to choose from, including some local treats.

After lunch, exit the hotel by its massive revolving doors to the riverfront. Opposite is **Cavenagh Bridge**, which was manufactured in Scotland and assembled in Singapore by Indian convicts in 1869. On the right-hand side of the bridge are bronze statues of five naked boys poised to jump into the river – a sport regularly practised by the children of Singapore's first immigrants. Called *First Generation*, it is the work of Singaporean sculptor Chong Fah Cheong. Further to the right is **Anderson Bridge**, built in 1910.

Return to the hotel, descend to its basement level and take the underpass that connects to the literally ship-shape **One Fullerton** building, a sleek restaurant and nightlife hub facing the sea off Marina Bay. Turn left and continue to the end, where the **Merlion Park** is located. The Merlion, Singapore's

tourism icon, has a lion's head, which recalls the myth of Singapore's original founder Sang Nila Utama, said to have spotted a lion when he landed in the 13th century – as well as a fish tail symbolising the island's beginnings as a fishing village.

Esplanade Theatre

From this vantage position, the impressive sight of the Esplanade – Theatres on the Bay is unmistakable, but first, take a cruise along the Singapre River. Buy a ticket (S$12) at the **Merlion Park Jetty** for the Singapore River Experience, a 30-minute cruise on a traditional 'bumboat'. Kick back and relax as the boat wends its way past Boat Quay to Clarke Quay and back, passing under several historic bridges. Disembark at the same jetty where you boarded the boat and continue with your walk. Take the stairs to the left of the Merlion Park and walk along **Esplanade Bridge** which runs beside Esplanade Drive. To the left you will see the soaring I M Pei-designed **Swissôtel the Stamford**, once the tallest hotel in the world but now supplanted by sky-piercing upstarts elsewhere.

The spiky silhouette of **Esplanade – Theatres on the Bay** (www.esplanade. com.sg) gave rise to much controversy when it was opened in October 2002. The pair of dome-shaped auditoriums have often been compared to the thorny shells of the *durian* by locals – whose smell and taste one either loves or hates. Unfortunately, the performance venue seems to have elicited a similar response. Still, it is an impressive sight, so try and catch a performance in either its massive 1,600-seat concert hall or the 2,000-seat theatre, both of which feature excellent acoustics. Designed by British architect Michael Wilford together with Singapore's DP Architects, the S$600-million facility hopes to be a cultural landmark along the lines of Sydney's Opera House.

At the end of Esplanade Bridge, turn right to the entrance of the Esplanade

Above: Esplanade – Theatres on the Bay

Theatre. The foyer is a little disppointing, given the grandiose exterior but there is always an art exhibition of some sort to liven up this cold and empty space. Make enquiries at the box office (daily noon–8.30pm) about shows you might like to see (the well-regarded Singapore Symphony Orchestra performs its concert season here and tickets are a steal at S$11 upwards). The theatre connects to the **Esplanade Mall**. Buy an ice cream cone at the Haagen Daaz outlet and have it at the waterfront facing the outdoor amphitheare at the ground level, then continue to Suntec City.

Suntec City

The next part of your walk is all underground (and thankfully air-conditioned). Descend to basement level and follow the signs to the MRT/CityLink Mall. Take the escalator up to the subterrannean **CityLink Mall** which connects all the way to **City Hall MRT Station** and **Raffles City** (if you turn left) and to **Suntec City** (if you turn right). If the retail outlets here don't distract you, walk to the end where an overhead bridge connects to Suntec City.

Conventions are an important business in Singapore, and the **Singapore International Convention and Exhibition Centre** at Suntec City has the advantage of size. It can accommodate 12,000 delegates in its column-free convention hall and has 12,000sq m (130,000sq ft) of space, supported by 1,000 IDD phone lines and a 12-language simultaneous interpretation system.

Suntec City also houses the massive **Suntec City Mall** linked to four office blocks. The entire design is based on the human hand, with the four tower blocks as fingers and the lower convention centre as the thumb. Most importantly, the ring-shaped **Fountain of Wealth** is held in the palm of the hand. Since water symbolises wealth, the significance is clear. The fountain is listed in the Guinness Book as the world's largest of its kind. The best views

Above: Singapore International Convention & Exhibition Centre. **Right:** the Fountain of Wealth

of the fountain are at street level, but to get up close, descend to the basement level. On the eastern flank of Suntec City is the luxurious **Conrad Centennial** hotel, which has several restaurants, including the elegant **Golden Peony** (tel: 6432 7482) for fine Cantonese food. An elevated pedestrian walkway connects Suntec City to the sprawling **Marina Square** shopping complex, which links three hotels: **The Oriental**, **Marina Mandarin** and the **Pan Pacific**, all of which have excellent restaurants. On the other side of Marina Square, the **Ritz-Carlton Millenia** is lavishly decorated with expensive works of art. Enjoying a drink amid the glow given off by the brilliant colours of a Chihuly glass sculpture at the lobby bar is a great way to end the day.

2. ORCHARD ROAD *(see map, p30–1)*

Shopping, like eating, are respected hobbies in Singapore. Spend the day cruising along this popular shopping strip; this is a chance to indulge in unabashed consumerism and instant gratification.

This entire route is well-served by buses, taxis and the train (with three MRT stations spanning the length). The shops do not open till about 10.30am, so if you wish, start off with an early morning stroll at the nearby Botanic Gardens (see page 46) and have breakfast at the Café Les Amis at the Visitor Centre, before a 10-minute stroll to Tanglin Mall on Tanglin Road

Tanglin Mall was opened in 1995 and quickly became a local favourite for its annual Christmas decorations, which feature a foam machine dispersing artificial snow on the pavement outside. Inside, Boon's Pottery (01-30) specialises in Singaporean ceramics, while Rustic Living (03-05) stocks handicrafts from the region, as does AkaMotif (01-01/02), a good choice for Indonesian silk batik.

You can also find sports, music and computer games shops within.

Continue past the arcades of Tudor Court, and move on to **Tanglin Shopping Centre**, a concentration of quality art galleries and antique shops. Follow the road round the corner of **Orchard Parade Hotel** – this is where **Orchard Road** proper begins.

Orchard Road is a die-hard shopper's dream come true – and a non-shopper's nightmare – lined with shopping complexes on both sides, with roadside refreshment stands and hotels with yet shopping arcades within. First off is **Forum The Shopping Mall**, which is filled with stores catering to children. On the ground floor is a string of restaurants, including a branch of celebrated San Francisco chain, **California Pizza**

Left: glittering Wheelock Place

Kitchen (tel: 6836 0110), and a **Coffee Bean** outlet.

The shopping arcade at the **Hilton Hotel** next door is a good stop for *haute couture* and designer jewellery. First, pass generals Wei Chi Jing De and Qin Shu Bao of the Tang dynasty, as they guard the hotel from the greenery of the driveway. Once in, you will find Miyake and Armani, among others. Opposite is the swanky **Palais Renaissance** for yet more designer-brand boutiques. On the same side of Hilton Hotel, after the ageing **Far East Shopping Centre**, is **Liat Towers**, where upstairs is the Spanish clothing store Zara, while luxury goods stores Hermès and Massimo Dutti are downstairs. The adjoining Starbucks is perpetually filled with teenagers nursing their iced lattés.

Next door, at the intersection of Orchard and Scotts roads is the sharp-pointed **Wheelock Place**, housing the massive **Borders** bookstore, which registered the highest sales worldwide on its first day of business here. Borders stocks a good selection of works by regional and Singaporean writers. For a vivid portrayal of Singaporean life in the 1950s, get a copy of *Clarence Plays the Numbers* by Yen Chung. To escape the bustle of Borders, head to **Epsite** (03-18; daily 11am–9pm; free; tel: 6736 4986), a serene, stylish gallery that showcases mainly digital imaging works and occasionally video art by artists from around the world. British retail institution **Marks & Spencer** (daily 10.30am–9.30pm; tel: 6733 8122) is on basement levels 1 and 2.

Detour into Scotts Road

Cross the road to **Shaw Centre**, at the corner with **Scotts Road**, which has Japanese department store **Isetan** (daily 10am–9.30pm; tel: 6733 1111), and floor upon floor of restaurants and shops selling everything from fine crystal to gym equipment. The **Lido Cineplex** within has eight screens. Singaporeans are among the world's greatest movie buffs – with each person averaging 7.2 films a year. Head down Scotts Road to the decidedly young **Pacific Plaza**, where teenagers hang out at its stores carrying funky streetwear and merchandise. That CD Shop, spanning two levels here, is well regarded for its inventory of hard-to-find chill-out and jazz titles at reasonable prices.

Past the **Royal Plaza Hotel** is a striking red building called DFS **Galleria**. The four-level temple to consumerism stocks an amazing variety of goods, from high-end clothing and accessories to a gourmet shop selling caviar and fine wines. Even if such things don't appeal, have a look at its ground level: the kitschy and very loud interior combining elements of Chinese, Indian and Malay décor stocks an array of touristy souvenirs for the folks back home.

Now take the overhead bridge to the other side, where another shopping trap awaits in the form of **Far East Plaza**. This mall has an offbeat character, catering to all age groups, while its basement level has shops which tar-

get trendy teens. The building has not worn its years well, but it is still a great place to shop, with lots of opportunities for bargain hunting.

Far East Plaza is flanked by two hotels which could not be more different. The more interesting of the two is the **Goodwood Park Hotel**, gazetted as a national monument in 1989. Built by Swan and MacLaren in 1900 as the Teutonia Club for German residents in Singapore, it was acquired by the British custodian of enemy property in 1914 when World War I broke out. The Japanese occupied it as military headquarters during the next world war, while the British military administration turned it into a war-crime court in 1945. The Goodwood's rusticated windows, ornamented façade and gables were retained in renovations in 1947 and 1959, but the original tower was removed. High tea at its **Café L'Espresso** (tel: 6730 1743) with its finger sandwiches and scones is an elegant affair.

On the other side of Far East Plaza is the **Grand Hyatt**, where the curiously angled doors of the hotel's main entrance and the Zen-looking fountain were installed after the building was renovated some years ago. The talk at the time was that these improvements were designed to address geomancy (*feng shui*) issues rather than out of practical considerations; and sure enough, the hotel prospered after these features were installed. Of course,

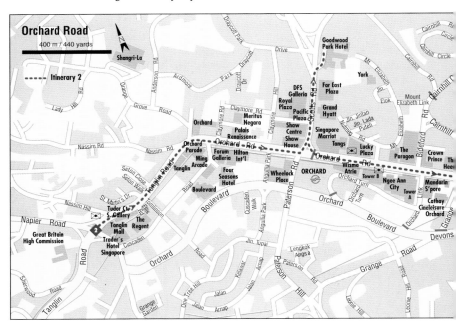

city itineraries

it could just be the elegantly luxurious ambience that attracts its clientele or its superb restaurants like **Mezza9** (tel: 6416 7189), where different menus from five open kitchens are served in the expansive dining area.

Tangs and more

At the junction of Scotts and Orchard roads is **Marriott Hotel**, which adjoins **Tangs** department store (Mon–Sat 10.30am–9.30pm, Sun 11am–8.30pm; tel: 6737 5500) with its Chinese green-tiled roofs. The family-run store was founded by patriarch C K Tang, who arrived in Singapore in 1922, and was the first to recognise the potential of Orchard Road. As a Christian, he was unconcerned by the presence of a Chinese cemetery opposite the store's location; in fact, business flourished and outgrew the original smaller building. Today, Tangs is an important landmark in the shopping precinct and its basement level connects to **Orchard MRT Station** opposite. The mosaic-tiled mural at the side of the station's entrance is a favourite backdrop for camera-clicking tourists.

Take a deep breath and soldier on along Orchard Road because there is no respite to the shopping. **Lucky Plaza**, the bargain-filled electronics goods haven, is next. On Sundays, it sees hundreds of Filipino domestic workers enjoying their day off work. Opposite is the striking blue-panelled **Wisma Atria** where another branch of the Japanese retail giant **Isetan** (daily 10am–9.30pm; tel: 6733 7777) is found, along with numerous smaller retail outlets and designer boutiques.

Just next door and linked by an underpass are the twin towers of the mega-mall **Ngee Ann City**, with a whole floor of restaurants and stores selling everything from *haute couture* to street fashion. **Takashimaya** department store (daily 10am–9.30pm; tel: 6738 1111) here has a wonderful food hall, purveying delicacies from the world over. **Kinokuniya** (Mon–Fri, Sun 10am–9.30pm, Sat 10am–10pm; tel: 6737 5021) on the third floor is a book-lover's dream with books in five languages – English, Chinese, French, German and Japanese. **Fourum** on level 4, dedicated to art galleries and stylish stationers, is also worth a browse.

Unbridled consumerism continues across the road at the **Paragon**, filled with designer boutiques. Past Bideford Road and Crown Prince Hotel is the **Heeren**, home to **HMV** music store and other teenager-friendly outlets. A popular **Spinelli's** café is on the ground floor.

Top left: historic Goodwood Park Hotel

Peranakan Place

Somerset MRT Station is close by, if you want to call it a day. But I would suggest a visit to the **Singapore Visitors Centre @ Orchard** (daily 9.30am– 10.30pm) at the junction of Cairnhill and Orchard roads. You can get information about attractions, purchase tickets to events, and book tours to nearby Malacca and Bintan (*see pages 64–70*) here. Thereafter, have a drink at **Peranakan Place** (tel: 6732 6966), a pedestrian area lined with colourful and highly ornamented Peranakan houses. Your choices include the ultra-cool **Acid Bar**, the atmospheric **Alley Bar** and the hip dance club **Rouge**; or just flop out at the sidewalk café **Rouge Outdoors**, great for people-watching.

Alternatively, head up **Emerald Hill**, the leafy stretch just behind Peranakan Place, to watering holes including **No 5** (tel: 6732 0818) and **Ice Cold Beer** (tel: 6735 9929). Emerald Hill is a quiet enclave of dignified and beautifully restored two-storey Peranakan dwellings facing each other across a communal space. The houses, built between 1901 and 1925, were the first to be given conservation status in 1981. The area is immortalised in local

writer Stella Kon's *Emily of Emerald Hill*, a one-woman play tracing the life of a Peranakan woman from child-bride to matriarch. It premiered in Singapore in 1985 and has been recognised as a landmark work in Singaporean theatre.

If you have the time and energy for more shopping, **Robinsons**, the oldest department store in Singapore, is at **Centrepoint**, while **John Little**, its contemporary, can be found just across the road in **Specialists' Centre**.

When ready for dinner, Centrepoint offers many choices. Or you can head to **Lei Gardens** (tel: 6734 3988) on the third level of **Orchard Shopping Centre**, next to the Specialists' Centre, for exquisite Cantonese food. **S-11 Cuppage Terrace**, next to Centrepoint, and its S11 Food Court is a good place for round-the-clock outdoor dining and drinking.

Beyond this area, the shopping pickings are slim. Just beyond Centrepoint is **Orchard Point**, where you can find the four-storey **OG** department store. Past Orchard Plaza and Le Meridien Hotel is the entrance to the **Istana**, the state residence of the President. Its sprawling grounds are open to visitors on some public holidays, and with luck you can catch the changing of the guard. Opposite is the leafy **Istana Park** with stunning orchid displays.

Plaza Singapura further on is another good place for a break or more shopping. Next door is **The Atrium@Orchard** with its transparent glass façade. **MacDonald House** – one of the oldest multi-storey office buildings in this area – and the adjoining buildings mark the end of Orchard Road. Just opposite The Atrium@Orchard and linked by an underpass is the huge **Dhoby Ghaut MRT Station**, so if you want to call it a day, this is your escape hatch.

city itineraries

3. THE CIVIC DISTRICT *(see map, p22)*

Travel back into time to see architectural jewels dating back to Singapore's colonial days. See historic civic buildings and museums, many restored and adapted from completely different functions in the past.

To get to the starting point, take the train to City Hall MRT Station and walk through Raffles City to Raffles Hotel. A taxi is usually a good alternative

You cannot visit Singapore and not stop by the famous **Raffles Hotel**, built by the Armenian Sarkies brothers in 1887. Through the years, famous personalities have stayed at Raffles – Somerset Maugham summed up its spirit best when he said that 'Raffles stands for all the fables of the exotic East'. Restored in the early 1990s, purists criticise the shopping mall extension to the hotel, but somehow, it all seems to blend in grand style. Stroll through the shopping arcade and enjoy the little courtyards with antique fountains.

History buffs may want to visit the small **Raffles Hotel Museum** (daily 10am–7pm; free; tel: 6337 1886) for memorabilia and the complete story of the hotel. Check to see if there are performances at the **Jubilee Hall** in the evening, or come back for dinner *(see page 56)*. Food enthusiasts can sign up for cooking lessons taught by the hotel's chefs at the **Raffles Culinary Academy** (tel: 6412 1256).

Leave the hotel by its splendid main entrance on Beach Road and turn right. Cross **Bras Basah Road** and walk past the **War Memorial Park** with its four 67-m (220-ft) tall columns, affectionately called 'chopsticks' by locals. The monument is dedicated to the 50,000 civilians who died in Singapore during World War II. On your right is the I M Pei-designed **Raffles City**, a vast complex comprising a shopping mall and two hotels – the striking 72-storey **Swissôtel the Stamford** and the adjoining 26-storey **Raffles the Plaza**.

Above: the elegant Raffles Hotel
Left: St Andrew's Cathedral

Beneath the complex is the busy **City Hall MRT Station**, which is linked underground to the subterranean CityLink Mall to both Suntec City and the Esplanade – Theatres on the Bay *(see pages 26–7)*.

Continue past **Stamford Road** and walk into the peaceful grounds of **St Andrew's Cathedral**. Indian convicts who built the cathedral used a special plaster made of egg white, egg shells, lime, sugar and coconut husk, known as Madras *chunam*. The cathedral is the second place of worship to be built on this site (the earlier Palladian-style building was demolished in 1852). The early English-Gothic style cathedral that you see now was designed by Ronald MacPherson and consecrated in 1862.

Around the Padang area

Leave the cathedral on the diagonal path towards the green expanse known as the **Padang**, or 'field'. In 1942, during the Japanese Occupation, European civilians were herded onto the Padang and forced to march more than 22km (14 miles) to Changi, where they were imprisoned. In 1945, Lord Louis Mountbatten accepted the Japanese surrender on the grand staircase of **City Hall** facing the Padang; and it was here too that Lee Kuan Yew declared Singapore's independence from Britain in 1959. These days, the Padang plays host to rugby and cricket matches, and the National Day parade on 9 August.

Next to the City Hall is the majestic green-domed **old Supreme Court**. Dating back to 1936, the figures on the façade are by Italian sculptor Rudolfo Nolli, who is said to have used his daughter as model. The old Supreme Court building is currently being converted into Singapore's National Gallery. Behind it stands the gleaming glass-and-steel **new Supreme Court**, capped by a dramatic circular disc.

On either side of the Padang are private clubs: the venerable,

Above: National Day parade at the Padang (with City Hall in the background)
Right: Sir Stamford Raffles statue at the Victoria Theatre

city itineraries

Victorian **Singapore Cricket Club** to your right, and the newer Singapore Recreation Club to your left.

Head towards the Singapore Cricket Club to the **Victoria Theatre** and **Concert Hall** with the landmark clock tower linking the two buildings and the original 1887 bronze **Statue of Stamford Raffles** in the forecourt. Although the two buildings were designed to match, Victoria Theatre, completed in 1862, predates the 1902-built Concert Hall (known as the Victoria Memorial Hall then). In the late 1970s, the latter was renovated to serve as a concert hall for the Singapore Symphony Orchestra and it remained so until 2003 when the orchestra moved to its new home at the Esplanade – Theatres on the Bay *(see page 26)*. The 883-seat Victoria Concert Hall with its classic shoebox-shape, still ranks as one of the best concert halls in Singapore. The Victoria Theatre door is a popular venue for theatre and lyric productions.

Next door is the **Asian Civilisations Museum** at Empress Place (Mon 1–7pm, Tues–Sun 9am–7pm, Fri 9am–9pm; admission fee; tel: 6332 7798; www.nhb.gov.sg/acm) which opened in February 2003. Designed by J F McNair, it was erected between 1864 and 1865 by convict labour, with new wings added in later years. After various stints as court house and government offices, major renovations were carried out in the late 1990s to convert the building into the Asian Civilisations Museum.

Be sure you devote enough time to this exceptional museum which encapsulates the history and cultures of East, Southeast, South and West Asia in its 10 galleries spread over three floors. Evocatively lit exhibits and computer-aided interactive stands help to explain the historical and cultural complexity of the different Asian civilisations. Exit by the **Museum Shop**, where you might want to pick up a memento of your visit. The river-side-facing side of the museum houses **Siem Reap II** (tel: 6338 1720), a restaurant serving Indochinese specialities and the trendy **Bar Opiume** (tel: 6339 2876) next door.

Continue by the river to another **Statue of Stamford Raffles** – this one a white marble replica of the original found outside the Victoria Theatre – marking the site of his first landing on 28 January 1819, and aptly named **Raffles' Landing Site**. Just opposite are the restored shophouses of **Boat Quay** *(see pages 24 and 85)* behind which rise the soaring office towers of Singapore's Central Business District.

Just adjacent, **The Arts House** (tel: 6332 6900; www.theartshouse.com.sg) occupies the premises of the Old Parliament House. Its 200-seat performance space called the Chamber was used by MPs to debate bills and laws in the past. Built by Coleman in the 1820s, the building was originally designed to be the private residence of a wealthy merchant. On its grounds sits the statue of a bronze elephant, a gift from King Chulalongkorn of Siam in 1871. Next

Above: China gallery at the Asian Civilisations Museum at Empress Place

door, behind high walls is somewhat austere new **Parliament House**.

Walk by the riverside to **Elgin Bridge**, where an underpass on its right will take you to **North Boat Quay**. Cross the road to **Hill Street**. You can't miss the startling multi-coloured shutters of the **Ministry of Information, Communications and the Arts**. This used to be the Hill Street Police Station, first erected in 1934. Several interesting art galleries are on the ground floor and occasional art exhibitions are presented in the atrium space.

Turn left as you come out and walk along Hill Street. To the left is a steep staircase that leads up to the **Fort Canning Park**. History abounds on this tree-covered bluff, once known as Bukit Larangan (Forbidden Hill) as commoners were not allowed here. Archaeological excavations indicate that the Malay princes who ruled Singapore in the 14th century had their grand palaces here. Realising that the hill offered a good vantage point to keep watch on Singapore's coastal waters, Raffles built his residence here in 1823, and in 1860, the British built a fort here from where dawn, noon and dusk each day were announced by cannon fire.

Museums and churches

Continue along Hill Street to the **Central Fire Station**, a fine example of the 'blood and bandage' style, alternating exposed brickwork and masonry. It now houses the **Civil Defence Heritage Gallery** (Tues–Sun 10am–5pm; free; tel: 6332 2996), a museum devoted to civil defence history. A gleaming red motorised steam fire engine that dates back to 1905 occupies pride of place here.

If you're an avid stamp collector, turn left up **Coleman Rise** to visit the the **Singapore Philatelic Museum** (Mon 1–7pm, Tues–Sun 9am–7pm; admission fee; tel: 6337 3888; www.spm.org.sg). If not, cross **Colemen Street** to the **Armenian Church of St Gregory the Illuminator**, the oldest church in Singapore and where Singapore's tiny Armenian community gathers on Sundays. Another building by Coleman, it was commissioned by the elders of the Armenian community in 1834. In the Memorial Garden is the tombstone of Agnes Joaquim, who discovered the orchid Vanda Miss Joaquim, now Singapore's national flower.

Exit the church and turn left at **Loke Yew Street** to Armenian Street's **Asian Civilisations Museum**, which is now closed for renovations. The original building was constructed by Hokkien immigrants to preserve their cultural heritage and to house the Tao Nan School, which was also the first school in Singapore to use Mandarin as the medium of instruction. The building will reopen in 2008 as a Peranakan museum. The Peranakan, or Straits Chinese, have a fascinating hybrid culture that evolved through years of intermarriage between immigrant Chinese men and local Malay women in the 19th century.

Above: remains of the old walls at Fort Canning Park

city itineraries

Next to it is **The Substation** (tel: 6337 7535; www.substation.org), an arts centre for artistic experimentation and cutting-edge work, converted from a disused power station. It has a tiny theatre and an equally tiny gallery, which connects to a charming garden overhung with trees. Located in the garden is **Timbre Music Bistro** (tel: 6338 8227), an atmospheric nook where Singapore bands and musicians perform nightly from Monday to Saturday.

Turn left from the Substation and walk along **Stamford Road**. On your right are the buildings of the **Singapore Management University**. Further along is the **National Museum** (daily 10am–6pm; admission fee; tel: 6332 5642; www.nationalmuseum.sg), which has history exhibitions and lifestyle-oriented events aplenty. The original building was designed by Major J F McNair and opened in Queen Victoria's Jubilee Year. Now, fresh from a major facelift, the museum boasts a new glass-and-steel wing with a 16-m (52-ft)-high glass rotunda. At night, the rotunda lights up like a lantern, with images that depict Singapore's history.

Cross Stamford Road into **Bencoolen Street** and turn right into **Bras Basah Road** where the **Singapore Art Museum** (daily 10am–7pm, except Fri 10am–9pm; admission fee; tel: 6332 3222; www.singart.com) is located. Housed in a former Catholic mission school, St Joseph's Institution, the 19th-century structure is an example of sensitive restoration. Apart from the permanent collection of some 4,000 Southeast Asian artworks, the museum also showcases special touring exhibits.

To end the day, continue to the corner of Bras Basah Road and Victoria Street to **Chijmes** (pronounced 'chimes'; www.chijmes.com.sg). This was the former Convent of the Holy Infant Jesus, founded by Rev Mother St Mathilde in 1854. The nuns ran a school for girls with boarding facilities and an orphanage which took in babies left on its doorstep. The old chapel with stained glass is now used for dinners and concerts, and speciality shops and restaurants fill the old cloister walkways. The restoration and conversion of the convent into a food and entertainment complex did not take place without controversy, but there is general agreement that the physical restoration was tastefully done: the mouldings in the chapel and along the walkway are especially beautiful, and the fountain courtyard provides a pleasant place to pause.

Finish the day with Modern European cuisine at **La Baroque** (B1-07; tel: 6339 3396) or enjoy Japanese food at **Sun Japanese Dining** (02-01; tel: 6336 3166), before you adjourn to **Father Flanagan's** (B1-06; tel: 6333 1418) for drinks. Then, dance the night away at **Insomnia** (01-21; tel: 6338 6883).

Right: Chijmes comes alive at night

4. CHINATOWN *(see map, p22)*

Wander around the Chinese heart of Singapore – filled with narrow streets and religious buildings which reveal a fascinating mix of cultures. This itinerary will take 4–5 hours to complete.

Take a taxi to Jamae Mosque at the corner of Mosque Street and South Bridge Road, or take SBS buses 7 or 61. Alternatively, the train stops at the nearby Chinatown MRT Station, where Jamae Mosque is a short walk away

Singapore's historical racial enclaves are a direct result of deliberate town planning in the early 1820s by Raffles. Today, Chinatown is something of an oddity; it has an Indian-Muslim mosque and a Hindu temple as two predominant landmarks. Start your walk on **South Bridge Road**, where **Masjid Jamae**, with its white twin towers stand. Built in 1826, it is one of three oldest Tamil Muslim mosques in the area. The façade and entrance are aligned with the road, but the interior is oriented towards Mecca.

Past **Pagoda Street**, in colourful contrast with its towering *gopuram*, is the **Sri Mariamman Temple**, built in 1823 by Naraina Pillai, who accompanied Raffles on his second visit to Singapore in 1819. If you happen to be there at the right time, witness brightly clad devotees offer *puja* (prayers) under the watchful images of the colourful ceiling frescoes. This is where the Thimithi, or fire-walking festival, takes place around July–August each year when celebrants tread red-hot embers in a state of trance.

Opposite the road is **Eu Yan Sang** at 269 South Bridge Road for Chinese tonics and herbs, available both in their original form and in handy bottled capsules. The respected company has been in the business of traditional medicines for over a century.

Turn right into **Smith Street** to the **Chinese Opera Teahouse** on your left at No 5 (Tues–Sun noon–5pm; tel: 6323 4862; www.ctcopera.com.sg). Have a cup of tea and a snack at traditional Chinese tables, under the display of opera costumes on the wall. Cantonese opera excerpts are performed on Friday and Saturday evenings between 7–9pm: you can dine while watching this centuries-old traditional theatre in action (bookings advised).

Part of Smith Street and the adjoining Trengganu and Pagoda streets have been closed to traffic and turned into a pedestrian mall. Street hawkers, albeit adhering to 21st-century sanitation standards, have made a comeback at

Chinatown Food Street at Smith Street. In the evenings, you can sample hawker favourites such as *char kway teow* (fried rice noodles) and Hainanese chicken rice here (daily 5–11pm). Another option is a visit to the **Chinatown Night Market** (daily 5–11pm), where Chinese handicrafts, opera masks and home accessories are on sale, and vanishing trades such as streetside fortune-telling and clog-making are back in business again.

At the corner with **Trengganu Street** is **Tzu Chi Foundation**. Formerly known as **Lai Chun Yen**, this is one of the earliest three-storey buildings in the area, with a verandah running around the top level. A former Chinese opera house dating back to the early 1900s, it is now occupied by a Buddhist association on the upper floor. Go up to the first floor to view the interior with its carved banisters and gleaming wooden floors and the stage where famous Chinese opera stars used to act.

On the opposite corner is **Chinatown Complex**, closed for upgrading until the end of 2007. It used to be one of the best places to experience local life, with a basement market where vendors sold seasonal fruit and vegetables, as well as fish, poultry and dried goods. Upstairs was a food centre with old-fashioned hawker fare. A temporary food centre has been set up across New Bridge and Eu Tong Sen roads near the Outram MRT Station.

Pagoda Street attractions

Alternatively, continue along Trengganu Street pedestrian mall area and pick up a Chinese *gong fu* outfit or brocade dressing gown – and don't be shy about bargaining. Turn left into **Pagoda Street** where tucked in between the many brightly-cloured shophouses in this area at No 46–50 is the **Chinatown Heritage Centre** (daily 9am–8pm; admission fee; tel: 6325 2878; www.chinatownheritage.com.sg). Using authentic furniture, utensils and other paraphernalia, the living conditions of the Chinatown of yesteryear are brought to life. Further down Pagoda Street you will be greeted by the aroma of barbecued meats, a must-have snack for the lunar new year, now available all year round from any of the **Bee Cheng Hiang** outlets with their bright red neon signs.

At the end of Pagoda Street, either take the overhead bridge across **New Bridge Road** to explore the warren of shops offering great buys in fabrics and clothes in **People's Park Complex**, or turn left and continue your walk along New Bridge Road, passing Lucky Chinatown, and turning left into **Keong Saik Road**.

Once famous for its brothels and bars, Keong Saik Road has been gentrified today. Some of the brothels are still there (look out for the

Left: Chinatown grocery shop **Above:** Sri Mariamman Temple
Right: Chinese herbal tea

red light at the front door) but many of the old buildings here have been renovated into boutique hotels, including the **Royal Peacock Hotel** at No 55 and
Hotel 1929 at No 50. The latter, built in 1929 naturally, is a hip hotel mixing
colonial architecture with chic art deco furniture. Its **Ember** restaurant (tel: 6347
1928) serves excellent Modern European cuisine with a light Asian touch.

Take a leisurely stroll around: turn left into **Jiak Chuan Road**, right at
Teck Lim Road and left into **Neil Road**, crossing to the opposite side to continue your walk. Turn right into **Duxton Road** where the area opens up into
a charmingly restored haven of old shophouses, with the dignified **Berjaya
Hotel** stands at No 83. The adjoining **Duxton Hill** is home to trendy PR
and media agencies, as well as a clutch of bars and restaurants.

Continue left into **Craig Road** and turn left into **Tanjong Pagar**, an area
with yet more restored shophouses. These narrow pastel-coloured two-storey
structures lend themselves to romantic dining with their ornate plaster façades,
wooden shutters, timbered floors and high ceilings.

At the junction of Tanjong Pagar and Maxwell roads is the popular **Maxwell
Food Centre**. Stop here to have a cheap local dinner before proceeding to the
junction of Tanjong Pagar and Neil roads, where **Jinriksha Station** is located.
In the early 1900s, *jinriks*, or human-powered rickshaws, were the main form
of transport. This was where rickshaws congregated in the past. Continue to **Tea
Chapter** (tel: 6226 1175) at 9A Neil Road for a refreshing cup of tea served
in a restful shophouse adorned with brush paintings and elegant screens.

5. ARAB STREET AND KAMPONG GLAM *(see map, p42)*

**Explore the area first established by Arab traders, and later the Malay
community. A late morning itinerary, ending with lunch.**

*Take a taxi to the Golden Landmark Hotel in Arab Street or the train to
Bugis MRT Station, from where the hotel is a short walk away*

The name **Kampong Glam** is derived from *kampung*, which means
village, and the Gelam tree, the *Melaleuca Leucadendron*, with spirally
arranged narrow leaves and white flowers. The bark was prized for its medic-

Above: Berjaya Hotel (formerly the Duxton) is located in the heart of Tanjong Pagar

inal values and was also used by the Bugis and Malays to caulk their ships. Despite the intentions of the colonial planners, the area shows a mix of the different ethnic groups that live and work in the area.

From the **Golden Landmark Hotel**, cross North Bridge Road into **Arab Street**, where a profusion of brocades and silk lines both sides. In addition to materials sold by the metre, you can pick up a batik wrap for S$6 or a silk *sari* with matching blouse for around S$200. Batik *sarong* with a contrasting panel, to be folded over the shoulder, can range from S$8 for machine-printed ones to S$400 for hand-drawn designs. At the corner with **Baghdad Street** is **Rishi Handicrafts** (No 58), its store front spilling over with baskets of every shape, size and colour, and colourful straw bags at a fraction of the prices downtown. Opposite, step into a more leisurely time in the dimly lit **Goodwill Trading** (No 56). Its walls are lined with batik, with a selection of pieces strung on poles for display, many of them in the S$18 range.

Proceed to **Beach Road**, and turn left past fishing tackle shops – a reminder that this was once the seafront. Turn left again at **Bussorah Street**, which during the Ramadan month – before the Muslim celebration of Hari Raya Puasa each year – is filled with street vendors selling delicacies for Muslims breaking their fast at sunset. At other times of the year, the street is quiet.

A Mall and a Mosque

Past the Baghdad Street junction, pause for a moment in the quiet pedestrian precinct of **Bussorah Mall**, flanked by restored 19th-century shophouses. On the left is the **House of Traditional Javanese Massage** (No 23; tel: 6298 9978). One of its more exotic massages uses a paste of ginger and herbs to remove excessive 'wind' from the body but you might want to opt for a less complicated foot massage instead. Opposite is

Jamal Kazura Aromatics (No 21) which sells a range of non-alcoholic essential oils like ylang ylang and lemongrass, as well as glass decanters to store these potions.

You are now in the heart of Kampong Glam. This quiet space offers a change of pace from the commerce of Arab Street to the spiritual values represented by the ornate **Sultan Mosque** (Sat–Thur 9am–noon, 2–4pm; tel: 6293 4405) just up ahead. The first mosque on this site was built in 1824 by Sultan Hussein Shah, who signed the treaty handing Singapore over to the British. The present mosque – the largest in Singapore – was designed by the colonial architectural firm of Swan and MacLaren, and was completed in 1928. The caretaker will direct you to leave your shoes outside.

Right: Sultan Mosque, Friday worship

Leave the mosque and turn left into **Kandahar Street** where the **Malay Heritage Centre** (Tue–Sun 10am–6pm, Mon 1–6pm; admission fee; tel: 6391 0450; www.malayheritage.org.sg) stands. It is housed in the former **Istana Kampong Gelam**, whose architecture combines traditional Malay motifs with the popular Palladian style dating back to the 1840s. It was once the palace of Sultan Ali Iskandar Shah, son of the first sultan of Singapore, Sultan Hussein. The museum has interesting displays pertaining to Malay history and culture. The adjacent two-storey **Gedung Kuning** (Yellow Mansion), built for Tengku Mahmoud, grandson of Sultan Hussein, is now the **Tepak Sireh Restaurant** (tel: 6396 4373).

A quick walk up Kandahar Street along the side of the Istana gets you to **North Bridge Road**. Turn right and three minutes away is **Sin Him Chuan Kee** at No 796-8 on the corner of **Aliwal Street**, which stocks buttons, ribbons, laces – almost anything you need to decorate a hat or deck out a bridesmaid. When you have had enough, go across North Bridge Road and up **Jalan Klapa** to **Victoria Street**. On your right and opposite are the golden domes of the blue-walled **Malabar Jama-Ath Mosque** (daily 10am–noon, 2–4pm; tel: 6294 3862). Next to it is the old **Malay Cemetery**, with graves arranged under sweet-smelling frangipani trees. Records dating from 1836 show that Malay princes are buried here.

Turn left along Victoria Street and enjoy the respite offered by trees along the walkway. At No 11 Jalan Pisang, make for **Hajjah Maimunah Restaurant** (tel: 6291 3132), an inexpensive self-service eatery serving traditional Malay food to nearby residents and office workers. Just point at the dishes you want to try, including the beef *rendang*, mildly spiced, tender and scented with lemongrass.

Back on Victoria Street, turn left, cross Ophir Road and the **Bugis MRT Station** is just ahead. Adjoining the station is **Parco Bugis Junction**, a huge glass-covered shopping mall with trendy boutiques and cafés.

Above: textiles of Arab Street
Right: Sri Veeramakaliamman Temple

Arab Street & Kampong Glam

400 m / 440 yards

Itinerary 5

city itineraries

6. LITTLE INDIA *(see map, p44)*

Serangoon Road is where immigrants from India first congregated, bringing their customs and lifestyles characterised by strong flavours and vibrant colours. Late morning is a good time to start.

Ask the taxi driver to take you to Tekka Centre at the corner of Serangoon Road and Rochor Canal Road, or take the train to the Little India MRT Station. Don't have breakfast as meal stops are included along this route

Tekka Centre, a popular market known for its low-priced fresh produce, has a maze of sundry shops on the upper level. The ground-floor food centre is a good place to start the morning with a milky ginger tea known as *teh halia*. The building is also known among locals as KK or Kandang Kerbau market, meaning 'buffalo pen' in Malay, recalling a time when abundant water and grass in the area made it especially conducive to cattle rearing. Street names in the area, such as Buffalo Road and Kerbau (Malay for 'buffalo') Road, also provide clues to its history.

Indian Delights

Serangoon Road has been described as the soul of Little India; shops in the vicinity cater to Singapore's minority Indian population, as well as visitors from India who come here regularly to shop. It is also a magnet for migrant workers from the Indian subcontinent who congregate here on weekends, especially on Sundays. At Deepavali, the whole area is lit up in celebration of the Festival of Lights and Singaporeans of all races come to eat, shop and join in the festivities.

Across Serangoon Road from Tekka Centre and a blight in this neighbourhood is the modern and multi-storey **Tekka Mall**. You get a better feel of the atmosphere at the pastel-coloured **Little India Arcade** next to it. Bounded by Hastings Road and Campbell Lane, there is a food court and stalls selling Indian jewellery, souvenirs, crafts, clothes and accessories. Exit by **Clive Street** where little shops are crammed with utensils and cookware, and return to Serangoon Road by **Campbell Lane**. In the arts and craft shops here, you will find carpets, furniture, incense holders, trinket boxes and statues of Buddha and Ganesh jumbled comfortably with Christian icons.

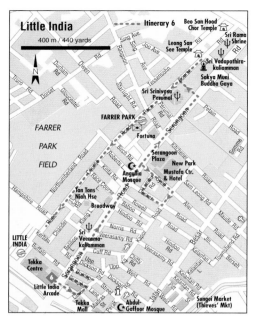

Little India

400 m / 440 yards

Lots of Colour

Opposite is **Jothi's Flower Stall**, where fragrant jasmine is strung up into garlands as offerings at Hindu temples. Continue right into Serangoon Road, which is dotted with restaurants, some of them established at a time when the area was largely populated by single men, whose domestic arrangements did not include a private kitchen. If you haven't yet had breakfast, head for the vegetarian **Ananda Bhavan** at No 58 Serangoon Road (tel: 6296 2105). It serves crispy *thosai*, a pancake made of rice and gram flour which can be eaten plain with a lentil gravy, or filled with *masala*, a spicy potato curry.

Turn right into **Dunlop Street** where you will see one of many provision shops in the area which feature heaps of fruits and vegetables spilling over onto the walkway in crates and baskets: onions and purple shallots, aubergines, tiny bitter gourds and betel leaf for chewing. There are packets of aromatic spices from bright yellow turmeric to deep red chilli, cloves, cinnamon sticks, whole nutmegs, cardamom pods, black peppercorns, strands of saffron and seeds of coriander, cumin, fennel and mustard.

When you've seen enough of Dunlop Street, backtrack to Serangoon Road and continue with your walk. Shops selling multi-coloured *sari* and ornate earrings, necklaces and bracelets line either side of Serangoon Road. Another Little India institution is **Komala Vilas** (No 76; tel: 6293 6980), serving spicy vegetarian fare and *thosai*. Keep your eyes peeled open for an itinerant – and elusive if the police are around – pavement fortune teller who uses a green parakeet to pick out a card that predicts your destiny.

Across the road, past **Belilios Road**, is the **Sri Veeramakaliamman Temple** (daily 5.30am–12.30pm, 4–9pm; tel: 6295 4538), one of the oldest Hindu temples in the area, dating from 1835. It is dedicated to the goddess Kali, the manifestation of anger against evil; she is shown ripping out the guts of a hapless victim. As consort to Shiva, Kali is also known as Parvati in her benign form; therefore she is both feared as well as loved. To the left of the temple, she is depicted flanked by Murugan, the child god, and Ganesh, the elephant god. You might see devotees circling the nine stones – representing the nine planets in the Hindu universe – arranged in a square at the far corner of the hall, or ringing a bell on the massive doors after prayers.

Right: Hindu religious statuary

Continue along Serangoon Road to **Birch Road**, where you will see another historic place of worship, the **Angullia Mosque**, built over 100 years ago. Cross over to the other side into **Syed Alwi Road** to visit the decidedly secular phenomenon that is **Mustafa Centre** (daily 24 hours; tel: 6295 5855). It stocks the widest selection of merchandise imaginable, heaped bazaar-style, and catering especially to visitors from the Indian subcontinent who come to purchase everything from toiletries to electronics. Amazingly, the store is opened 24 hours a day, and its enterprising owners have even gone e-commerce with purchases that can be made via the Internet. The owner's success has spawned further off-shoots of the Mustafa brand, including a hotel, a café and a travel agent, plus a new extension of the mall across at Verdun Road.

After you have braved the hordes at Mustafa's, turn right into **Kampong Kapur Road** (where the garish Royal India Hotel stands) and right again into **Desker Road**. This street has a somewhat seedy reputation and plenty of cheap hotels. Turn right into **Lembu Road**, where Indian migrant workers in the construction industry congregate at the **Lembu Road Open Space**. The sense of community is palpable as the characters drift in and out.

More Hindu Temples

Turn left into Syed Alwi Road and make your way back up to Serangoon Road. It's a good 10-minute walk to the next place of interest. After passing Fortuna Hotel and the Kitchener Road junction, cross to the opposite side (after Perumal Road) to the brightly coloured **Sri Srinivasa Perumal Temple** (daily 6.30am–noon, 6–9pm; tel: 6298 5771). It was founded by migrant Naradimhaloo Naidu, who endowed a portion of his property to the temple in 1860. A century later, local philantrophist P Govindasamy Pillay met the expenses for adding the five-tier *gopuram* or main tower, which rises 21m (70ft) over the entrance. Figures on the *gopuram* depict the various incarnations of Vishnu, also known as Perumal, the Preserver of Life, who appears on earth from time to time in different forms.

Each year, at Thaipusam, around January–February, a procession of devotees begins at the Sri Srinivasa Perumal Temple and winds up at Chettiar Temple in Tank Road. The men pierce their tongues, cheeks and bodies with skewers to support their *kavadi*, great arched steel structures decorated with peacock feathers. Women participate in the procession carrying jugs of milk on their heads. These acts of faith are performed either as penance or in gratitude to Lord Murugan, Shiva's son.

Leave the temple and follow the grassy path just next to it past blocks of public housing and a tiny playground. It will take you to **Race Course Road**, and to your right, the Chinese **Sakya Muni Buddha Gaya Temple** (daily 8am–4.45pm; tel: 6294 0714), also known as the Temple of 1,000 Lights

Right: Sakya Muni Buddha Gaya Temple

because the 15-m (50-ft)-high statue of the Buddha is surrounded by a halo with that many light bulbs. Inside the door is part of a branch of the sacred *bodhi* tree under which the Buddha is said to have attained enlightenment. Worshippers may illuminate the lights around the statue for a small donation. There is also an enlargement of the Buddha's footprint, inlaid with mother-of-pearl. Further down the road on your left are some lovely old houses and the Taoist **Leong San See Temple** (daily 6am–6pm; tel: 6298 9371) at No 371 with an ornately carved roof. The temple is dedicated to Kuan Yin, the Goddess of Mercy.

Once you're done, take a taxi down Race Course Road to the popular **Muthu's Curry** (No 138; tel: 6392 1722) for their potent fish head curry with eggplant, tomato and pineapple chunks, or equally good mutton chop or masala chicken. Order a glass of fresh lime juice to douse the fire. Alternatively, take the train one stop from nearby **Farrer Park MRT Station** to the **Little India MRT Station** where the restaurant is a short walk away.

7. BOTANIC GARDENS (see map, p52)

This lovely green lung is just minutes away from the noise and crowds of Orchard Road. There are formal gardens, virgin jungle, a fabulous orchid garden, and free concerts at Symphony Lake. Recommended as an early morning activity as you can have breakfast at the gardens, unless you intend to catch a weekend concert in the late afternoon.

The main Tanglin Gate entrance to the Botanic Gardens is at the junction of Holland Road and Cluny Road but this tour starts at its Nassim Gate entrance further along Cluny Road. Get to the closest train station at Orchard MRT and take a taxi from there, making sure that the driver drops you off at the Visitor Centre at Nassim Gate

The first Botanic Gardens in Singapore was established in 1822 to evaluate crops for commercial cultivation, the most successful example being the Para Rubber (*Hevea brasiliensis*) from Brazil introduced by Henry Ridley, who later went on to establish Malaya's lucrative rubber industry. The original park was closed in 1829.

The present **Botanic Gardens** (daily 5am–midnight; free; tel: 6471 7361; www.sbg.org.sg) was founded by an agri-horticultural society in 1859 and subsequently handed over to the government for maintenance. It contains over 3,000 species of trees and shrubs, in areas as varied as virgin jungle, marshland, lakes and formal gardens, and is a centre for horticultural and botanical research and experimentation, with a special emphasis in orchid breeding and hybridisation. The success of the orchid programme can be traced back to the 1920s when Eric Holtum was director of the gardens.

Top: *masala dosai*, a southern Indian staple
Right: the orchid garden at Botanic Gardens

In line with the research and educational mission of the gardens, most trees are clearly labelled, so you learn as you go along. Look out for the *couroupita guianensis* or Cannonball tree with hardy bright pink flowers and large heavy fruit hanging from the trunk, and the *lecythis ollaria* or Monkey pot, which opens a lid to release its seeds when ripe.

The 52-ha (130-acre) gardens is mostly empty on weekdays, a perfect time to visit for a bit of solace. On weekends however, scores of families and Filipino maids on their day off from work descend on the park. A lovely breakfast spot is **Café Les Amis** (tel: 6467 7326) which serves a selection of Asian and Western breakfast favourites. If you're there on the weekend, you may want to try the more lavish breakfast buffet spread at **Halia** (tel: 6476 6711) where you eat outdoors at tables set on a wooden deck.

Orchids Galore

After breakfast, make your way up **Palm Valley** to the **Orchid Plaza** and the entrance to the **National Orchid Garden** (daily 8.30am–7pm; admission fee), which houses a **Cool House** that encloses a montane tropical forest. The landscaped grounds of the Orchid Garden are filled with a profusion of orchids and given the 700 species of orchids and 2,100 hybrids found here, it is not surprising that only a handful will be recogisable to the non-horticulturalist. Meandering paths and Victorian gazebos make this a particularly charming walk. Don't miss the spectacular floral display in the mist room; and also visit Burkhill Hall, where you can view the *Dendrobium* Margaret Thatcher, or *Dendrobium* Benazir Bhutto and contemplate the similarities between these blooms and the personalities they have been inspired by and named after.

Take the **Lower Ring Road** after your visit to the Orchid Garden and you will come across the delightful *Girl on a Bicycle* sculpture zooming down the top of a manicured hedge. Further along is the *Girl on a Swing* and *Lady on a Hammock,* all by sculptor Sydney Harpley, and donated to Singapore by David Marshall, Singapore's First Chief Minister (1955–56). Swing right when you come to the **Swiss Granite Fountain** and walk past the **Sundial Garden** to **Swan Lake**. The **Marsh Garden** at one end will take you towards **Minden Gate**, where you exit onto Holland Road. Alternatively, take the road on the left at the fountain and walk through landscaped gardens to reach the **Botany Centre**, where you can stop at the **Taman Serasi Food Garden** for a refreshing fruit juice before you exit onto Cluny Road.

Early morning is a good time to visit the park, as are late afternoons at the weekends, especially when there are concerts on Symphony Lake.

Right: orchids in full bloom

8. HISTORICAL CHANGI *(see map, p48)*

Visit the memorial to prisoners of World War II at the Changi Museum
and then stroll around sleepy Changi Village for a taste of a quieter
slice of Singapore. Recommended as a half-day option.

*The easiest way is to take a taxi to the Changi Chapel on Upper Changi Road
North and ask the driver to wait while you visit, before continuing to Changi
Village. An alternative is to take the train to Tanah Merah MRT Station and
change to SBS bus 2. Guided tours are available for S$8 per person*

The chapel at the **Changi Museum** (daily 9.30am–5pm; free; tel: 6214
2451; www.changimuseum.com), on Upper Changi Road North, is a replica
of one of many similar places of worship built by prisoners of war while incarcerated in Changi Prison during the Japanese Occupation of Singapore from
1942 to 1945. Many such places were destroyed by the Japanese. The original of this example was dismantled after World War II and re-assembled
in Australia. The replica was jointly built by the tourism authorities and
the Singapore Prison Service in 1988 in response to interest by former prisoners of war and their families.

For years, the chapel stood inside the grounds of the old Changi Prison.
In contrast with the forbidding-looking prison edifice, the chapel sat in a garden with hibiscus and frangipani. Cards recording memories and gratitude
were affixed on a board to the left of the altar and visitors were invited to pick
a flower from the garden and place it on the altar in remembrance of the
men and women who suffered during the war. In February 2001, the chapel
was dismantled and re-consecrated on a new ½-ha (1.3-acre) site just 10
minutes from its original location, as part of a new museum.

A replica of the **Changi Murals**, life-sized portrayals of scenes from the
life of Christ, is also displayed in this new location. The originals in Changi
Prison were painted by bombardier
Stanley Warren of the 15th Field
Regiment while he was recover-
ing from serious injuries. The
Japanese military had given per-
mission for one of the prison wards
to be used as a chapel, which Warren decorated. For many years, the
ward was used as a store room, and
the murals lay hidden and forgot-
ten. They were discovered by the
Singapore Armed Forces only
years later during renovations. A
search for the artist ensued and
Warren was finally located in London. He was persuaded to return
to Singapore in 1963 and again in
1982 to complete its restoration.

The site of the original murals is
located within an operational mil-

Changi
800 m / 880 yards
- - - Itinerary 8
N

itary camp – Block 151 of Changi Airbase – and open for public viewing only during four window periods in February, August, September and November. Visitors wishing to view them must apply at least two weeks ahead to the public relations department of the Ministry of Defence (tel: 6768 3539).

The museum also provides moving insights into life as a prisoner of war in Changi Prison, which housed as many as 3,000 prisoners at one time. The stirring images on display include drawings by W R M Haxworth and photographs by George Aspinall. Among the war-time memorabilia are items donated by former prisoners of war and their families.

Changi Village

There is one more site to visit before we put the war behind us. Continue by taxi to **Changi Village**, and go down Lorong Bekukong opposite the Le Meridien Changi Village. Go past the market and take the footbridge across Sungei Changi. Continue past the Changi Sea Sports Club and the SCDF Sea Training Centre and you will be on **Changi Beach**, close to the **Changi Massacre Site**, where the sand was reported to have run red with blood during the brutal Japanese Occupation.

Look out over the water and allow the traffic in Serangoon Harbour and the boats at the mouth of Sungei Changi to bring you back to contemporary Singapore. Crossing the footbridge returns you to **Changi Point Ferry Terminal**, where you can catch a boat to Pulau Ubin (see *page 62*).

Alternatively, walk back to the sleepy village, past the coffee shops and food courts to the air-conditioned café at the **Le Meridien Changi Village**. If not head to the **Changi Village Hawker Centre**, where foodies recommend Wing Kee for *its hor fun* or flat rice noodles in beef or seafood gravy, or the *nasi lemak*, coconut rice served with fried fish, peanuts, egg and a spicy *sambal* sauce at stall No 57. Otherwise head for No 8, **Charlie's Corner** (Tues–Sun 11.30am–2.30pm, 6pm–midnight; tel: 6542 0867) for great burgers, fried chicken wings and potato wedges. Charlie's is something of a Changi institution, made famous by his enormous selection of icy cold beers from all over the world.

Above: the chapel at Changi Museum

9. JURONG BIRDPARK *(see map, p52)*

Nature lovers will revel in this extraordinary park devoted to birds. When you arrive, you will hear the calls of the birds even before you see them. Plan to spend the morning touring the park, finishing up with lunch by the lake where hundreds of pink flamingoes roost.

Take a taxi, or the train to Boon Lay MRT Station and transfer to SBS bus 194 or 251. Get there as early as possible to avoid the noon-day sun

The 20-ha (49-acre) **Jurong BirdPark** (2 Jurong Hill; daily 9am–6pm; admission fee; tel: 6265 0022; www.birdpark.com.sg) is home to some 8,000 birds from 600 different species from all over the world. Acknowledged as one of the leading bird parks in the region, the park attracts over a million visitors each year. Attractions include Parrot Paradise, Pelican Cove and Jungle Jewels walk-in aviary. One of the first exhibits you'll see is the **Penguin Parade**, where endearing penguins live and play in an environment similar to that of the South Pole. Glass enclosures allow visitors to watch some 200 penguins and 50 compatible seabirds such as inca terns and puffins.

Feathered Shows

The **Fuji World of Hawks show** at 10am features magnificent condors, falcons, owls and other birds of prey. After the show, you might like to visit the **Falconry Museum**. The **All Stars Birdshow** at the Pools Amphitheatre provides more entertainment at 11am and 3pm. Other fascinating bird shows held include the 11.45am **Hornbill Chit Chat** at the Hornbill Exhibit and the 1pm **Parrots Children's Show** at the Songbird Terrace. With so many free shows included in your admission ticket, check the show times and plan your route accordingly.

   Alternatively, just wander around the meticulously landscaped grounds, or hop onto the Panorail for dramatic views of the park along the 1.7-km (1-mile) long route. The elevated people-mover is an easy way to cover much of the park in air-conditioned comfort.

Above: tourist posing with macaws at Jurong Bird Park

Two outstanding attractions are the **Parrot Paradise**, a collection of 500 parrots from over 100 species, and the **Southeast Asian Birds Aviary**, a walk-through area of lush rainforest with the world's highest man-made waterfall, complete with a tropical thunderstorm at noon. Look out for feeding areas where fruit is placed in the trees for the free-roaming birds. They will be easy to spot for the colour and flurry of activity around these spots.

For lunch, the **Flamingo Café** offers an international menu of Asian and Western dishes, to be enjoyed while watching flights of pink flamingo – there are over 300 on the lake – through the floor-to-ceiling windows. Or have a quick meal at **Bongo Burgers**, an African-themed eatery serving gourmet burgers, pasta, and fish and chips.

10. BUKIT TIMAH NATURE RESERVE *(see map, p52)*

Highly urbanised Singapore retains pockets of rich primary rainforest within easy access of the city. A good example is the Bukit Timah Nature Reserve. You can enter the reserve earlier than the official hours; best as a morning excursion and expect to spend one to three hours.

Allow about 30 minutes to get there from town. From Newton MRT Station, buses No 67, 170, 171 will take you to Upper Bukit Timah Road, from where you have to walk up Hindhede Road and straight on to Hindhede Drive. A taxi is by far the easiest way. Have the driver drop you off at the car park. Wear a pair of shorts and t-shirt and liberally spray scent-free insect repellent

Located almost in the centre of Singapore is **Bukit Timah Nature Reserve** (daily 7am–7pm; free; tel: 6468 5736; www.nparks.gov.sg), which offers 164 ha (405 acres) of ecologically important lowland rainforest, and has Singapore's highest point at the top of **Bukit Timah Hill**, at 164m (538ft) above sea level.

Declared as a forest reserve back in 1884, the reserve has suffered significant changes both in its demarcated boundaries and biodiversity levels due to poaching of timber and animals in the early 20th century and more recent urban encroachments. There are no more large mammals like tiger and barking deer to be found and neither are there ecologically rare birds like hornbills and trogons, once part of the virgin rainforestscape. Still, nature lovers will not go away disappointed: there are over 2,000 recorded native plants and 170 species of fern. Do not expect to find the plants that feature in Singapore's urban greenery; most of those are imported species. Here is the real thing: you are looking at Singapore as she was in her earliest days. The wildlife in the park, too, is of an impressive variety, with 2 million insects and invertebrates, some 660 spiders, and 126 species of birds. A few small mammal species have survived too like squirrels, anteaters and treeshrews.

Right: weekend warriors at Bukit Timah Nature Reserve

Walk the Trails

In the early morning you can join fitness buffs jogging up the hill. The **Visitor Centre** (daily 8am–6pm) at the foot, is a good place to start. Orientate yourself and check out the different routes, which are clearly marked on the map at the entrance. You will also find these maps and directional signs along the trails. You can get to the summit and back in under an hour, taking the shortest route at a brisk pace, or spend up to 3 hours to cover more of the reserve. In wet weather, some of the paths can be a bit muddy and involve scrambling over fallen tree trunks – all part of the fun if you are prepared for it; and the variety of fungus that pop up just about everywhere is ample reward.

The first part, straight up the paved road can be discouraging, but once past this, you are in primary rainforest complete with a heavy canopy at the uppermost layer, rattans and liana vines at mid-level and red ginger flowers and dark purple bat lilies on the forest floor. Soaring dipterocarp trees are a feature of this reserve where there are more than 25 key species to be found.

Wildlife includes long-tailed macaque monkeys, black-and-white tree nymph butterflies, and hosts of birds including the racquet-tailed drongo with its distinctive percussive call. Take time to pause and listen to the variety of bird song, usually in full chorus in the morning. Look out for any fruiting trees – figs in particular – around which birds will flit and feast.

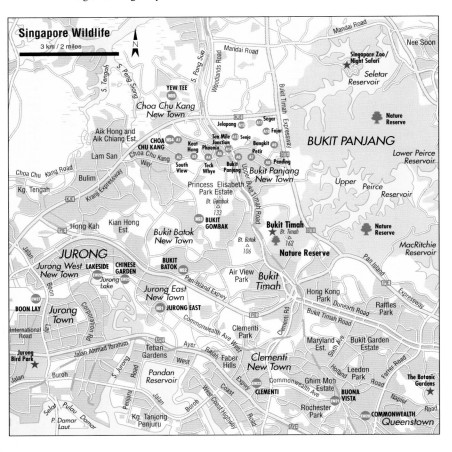

At the summit, enjoy the view of **Seletar Reservoir** to the north and the surrounding protected rainforest. Flooded old quarries resembling scenic Guilin in China is another attraction and a somewhat unexpected sight.

Before you leave, check out **Nature's Desire** (tel: 6467 8341), the gift shop at the Visitor Centre, for books on nature and souvenirs. On leaving Hindhede Drive, cross the main road on the overhead bridge to Cheong Chin Nam Road, which is lined with eateries. Have some coffee and *prata*, fluffy Indian pancake with curry, or a glass of soy milk with Chinese *yu char kway* (fried crullers).

11. CRUISE TO SOUTHERN ISLANDS *(see map, p54)*

Mingle with 'bumboats', the local water-taxis, and ocean-going craft in the busy harbour; take a day or evening cruise around the Southern Islands and sail past one of the busiest container ports in the world.

If you are going on Eastwind's cruise, take a taxi to Marina South Pier (31 Marina Coastal Drive) or catch the train to Marina Bay MRT Station and board bus service 402 to get to the pier. Watertours' cruises depart from the Singapore Cruise Centre at the HarbourFront Centre. Travel there by taxi or by train, stopping at the HarbourFront MRT Station

Several operators run harbour cruises, and you can usually get a ticket and board one of the daytime cruise boats about 15 minutes before departure. Dinner cruises, however, require advance bookings. **Eastwind** (tel: 6532 4740; www.fairwind.com.sg) operates two daytime cruises (10.15am and 3pm) on its *Fairwind* Chinese-style junk boat (S$20). **Watertours** (tel: 6533 9811; www.watertours.com.sg) has a tour (10.30am and 3pm) on the *Cheng Ho*, an ornate floating Chinese pavilion with traditional tiered roof-tops and golden dragons on the prow (S$25). Both cruises take about 2½ hours, and include a stop at Kusu Island; light refreshments are served on board. *Fairwind* operates a buffet dinner cruise at 6pm (S$36), while *Cheng Ho*'s Imperial dinner cruise (S$53) leaves at 6.30pm. Dinner cruises do not stop and last about 2 hours.

Above: the *Cheng Ho* Chinese junk

As you depart on the Eastwind cruise, you can enjoy the views of the city skyline with the spiky domes of the Esplanade – Theatres on the Bay and the soaring glass-and-steel towers of the Central Business District. Sail past Benjamin Sheares Bridge to the Eastern Anchorage, where as many as 300 ships from all over the world may be seen, giving a glimpse of what makes Singapore one of the world's busiest ports. If you are on the Water-

tours cruise, you will pass by Sentosa's coastline and enjoy views of the lush Labrador Park.

Southern Islands

Your cruise will dock in the narrow strait between Lazarus Island and **Kusu Island**. On Kusu – which in the past has been called Governor's Island by the Spanish, Goa Island by the British and Pulau Tembuku by the Malays – is **Tua Pek Kong Temple**, to which Chinese devotees flock every year for their annual pilgrimage in the ninth lunar month. The temple has classical Chinese green-tiled roofs and red walls and is reached via a series of pavilion-studded bridges set over a picturesque lagoon ringed with traveller's palms. In acknowledgement of the legend that the island was a turtle which transformed itself into a rock to save shipwrecked sailors, there is a turtle sanctuary as well as a pair of giant marble turtles. On the return trip, see the dense vegetation and the narrow strips of beach on **Lazarus Island** which offer a dramatic contrast to the organised and carefully groomed landscape of Kusu.

The cruise then continues past **St John's Island**, formerly used as a quarantine area for those with communicable diseases and later as a drug detention centre. It is now a holiday island. Beyond St John's are the twin mounds of **Sisters Island**.

On the horizon are the islands of Indonesia, while closer is the island of **Pulau Bukom**, home to oil refineries. Turning back, the boat sails past the hotels and golf clubs on **Sentosa** (see *page 59*), with the Merlion statue in the background.

As you approach the harbour, and your cruise passes the busy container terminal, you will be able to see some of the infrastructure that makes Singapore the number one port in the world.

Above: Tua Pek Kong Temple grounds
Right: Singapore Zoological Gardens

Cruise to Southern Islands
2 km / 1.2 miles

REDHILL · CLARKE QUAY · CITY HALL · TIONG BAHRU · CHINATOWN · Singapore River · Merlion · RAFFLES PLACE · OUTRAM PARK · Marina City Park · Mt. Faber 105 · Keppel Viaduct · TANJONG PAGAR · MARINA BAY · Mt. Faber Scenic Park · HARBOURFRONT · HarbourFront Centre · Keppel Harbour · P. Brani · Brani Shoals · Tg. Pagar · Selat · Sengkir · Mt. Serapong 85 · Eastern · Sentosa · Anchorage · P. Tekukor · Renggit · Selat Tampang Hakim · Tua Pek Kong Temple · Lazarus · Kusu · St. John's Island · Sisters Island · ::::: Itinerary 11

12. Daylight Zoo and Night Safari *(see map, p52)*

Spend an afternoon watching wild animals roam in the open in their natural habitats at the Singapore Zoological Gardens and when night falls, view nocturnal wildlife prowl in the moonlight at the unique Night Safari.

Take a taxi or SBS bus 138 from Ang Mo Kio MRT Station, or TIBS bus 927 from Choa Chu Kang MRT Station. The zoo and safari park are located next to each other at 80 Mandai Lake Road

An outing to the zoo to see animals behind bars is probably not most people's idea of fun but the zoo in Singapore is quite a different experience altogether. Bordering Seletar Reservoir, the 90-hectare (22-acre) **Singapore Zoo** (daily 8.30am–6pm; admission fee; tel: 6269 3411; www.zoo.com.sg) is tucked into the edge of a rainforest and displays some 3,000 animals, representing 200 species of wildlife. This is an open zoo, where most of the animals are kept in enclosures approximating their natural habitat, with no visible barriers. Animals are separated from visitors and each other by water moats and other concealed or low barriers for unobstructed views. See pygmy hippos wallow in their riverine environment while polar bears swim in an air-conditioned Arctic environment. Gibbons and spider monkeys leap through trees, and rhinos share space with antelopes in a recreation of the African plains.

A Wild Breakfast

The zoo boasts the world's largest colony of orang utan, the result of a very successful breeding programme. There is a chance to have a meal in close proximity to these adorable primates and other wildlife, including snakes and otters, at its daily **Jungle Breakfast** (daily 9–10am at the **Jungle Flavours** restaurant). Call ahead to make reservations. Animal shows featuring reptiles, primates, elephants and sea lions are staged several times a day at the open-air amphitheatre. Animal feeding times are posted at the zoo entrance, with the most spectacular feasts at the polar bear and lion enclosures.

One of the most popular attractions is the **Fragile Forest**, which highlights the interplay between animals and plants in the rainforest. The first zoo exhibit in the world to display invertebrates and vetebrates under one roof,

the Fragile Forest features a walk-in flight area – with fauna as diverse as tamarins, lemurs, sloths, parakeets and butterflies and four centres showing various ecosystems.

When the zoo closes at 6pm, take a break at the **Ulu Ulu Restaurant** (tel: 6269 3411) at the Night Safari. This casual eatery offers a variety of cuisines from Asia amid a rustic *kampung* (village) setting. If you are in the mood for ice cream, **Ben & Jerry's Scoop Shop** has a range of tempting flavours.

The Night Safari

Billed as one of a kind in the world, the 40-ha (99-acre) large **Night Safari** (daily 7.30pm–midnight; admission fee; tel: 6269 3411; www.nightsafari.com.sg) is set in dense tropical rainforest, and allows visitors to view nocturnal wild animals in their natural habitats. If you have been disappointed with disinterested big cats in ordinary zoos, it could be because almost 90 percent of tropical mammals are only active at night. At the Night Safari, these animals are seen at their most active: feeding, socialising and prowling in all their natural grace. Travelling by tram, you will see creatures like the Indian rhinoceros, striped hyena, golden jackal and majestic tigers. Altogether, some 1,200 animals of over 110 species roam the grounds of the park, unobtrusively lit so that the animals are not disturbed.

The overall effect is of a moonlit night and the thing to do is to keep absolutely quiet and let yourself be part of the surroundings, keeping your attention on observation rather than conversation. You will have a more enjoyable experience that way, as you encounter different types of terrain, from realistic recreations of Himalayan foothills to savannah grasslands. Flash photography is prohibited and, as the tram moves along, your guide points out animals coming into view in hushed tones. Walking trails are clearly marked and there are rangers stationed along the way to guide you.

13. RAFFLES REVISITED *(see map, p22)*

Drinks at the New Asia Bar, perched on the 71st floor of the Swissôtel the Stamford, followed by an elegant dinner at the historic Raffles Hotel.

Take the train to City Hall MRT Station and exit to the Swissôtel Stamford, making your way to the special lift that services the top-floor New Asia Bar. A taxi is a good option, especially if you are dressed up for the evening

The **Swissôtel the Stamford** (formerly known as the Westin Stamford) once held the record for being the tallest hotel in the world – until it was displaced by newer rivals. For the moment, however, it is still the tallest hotel in Southeast Asia. Make your way to the lobby of the hotel where an express lift will zip you 70 storeys to the pinnacle. On arrival, walk past the chic

Above: breakfast with unusual company at the zoo

Equinox restaurant one floor up to the equally plush **New Asia Bar** (tel: 6431 5669; www.equinoxcomplex.com). Order a lychee martini and be prepared to be stunned by the eye-popping views from this vantage point, with the city skyline all awash with lights. The New Asia Bar turns into a popular club after 10pm with a DJ playing dance music at the console.

Feed at the Raffles

After drinks, head towards the peaceful courtyards and ornate buildings of the **Raffles Hotel** (tel: 6337 1886) at Beach Road, where the 'Grand Old Lady of the East' presides. Restored to something far grander than its 1920s chic, the Raffles Hotel – whose elegant façade by now will be glowing against the gathering dusk – is still the most romantic place to dine in Singapore.

Follow Rudyard Kipling's advice and 'feed at the Raffles when visiting Singapore'. Your options are numerous. There is elegant dining in the best traditional style at **Raffles Grill**, often with visiting stellar chefs in command in the kitchen; imaginative fusion creations at **Doc Cheng's**, where platters tend to be sculpted glass pieces; the **Tiffin Room**, which recalls the best from the days of the Raj with its array of curries; the **Royal China**, which serves delicate Cantonese food; and the **Long Bar Steak House** where generous portions of the finest cuts of aged beef are served.

End the evening with a quiet drink at the **Bar & Billiard Room**, which carries a nice selection of cigars, and still houses the very billiard table under which the last tiger in Singapore, or so the story goes, is said to have been shot. For something less formal, head for the raucous **Long Bar**, the only place in Singapore where you can toss peanut shells onto the floor with impunity and not have the waiter bat an eyelid.

Above: Raffles Hotel courtyard
Right: Raffles Hotel shopping arcade

Excursions

1. SENTOSA *(see map, p61)*

Sentosa is the largest of Singapore's offshore isles, with a mind-boggling range of theme park-style attractions. Plan an entire day or stay overnight.

It's near impossible to see all of Sentosa's attractions in a single day, so this itinerary only covers some of the highlights. If you're inspired to see more, stay overnight at one of the island's hotels. For this itinerary, take The Sentosa Resort & Spa's complimentary shuttle bus from HarbourFront Centre (Jardine Steps), within walking distance from the HarbourFront MRT Station. The first shuttle leaves HarbourFront Centre at 8am, and every half an hour thereafter; tell the driver you are having breakfast at the resort. It is also possible to get to Sentosa by cable car (daily 8.30am–11pm, tel: 6270 8855), by Sentosa Bus (Sun–Thur 7am–11pm; Fri, Sat and eve of public holidays 7am–12.30am; $1 fee) from HarbourFront Centre Bus Terminal, or by taxi or private car. A basic admission ticket (S$2) includes entry to the park areas and beaches, and all transportation on the island. Most of the individual attractions have separate admission fees but there are also 'package' tickets with entrance to multiple attractions. Call 1800-736 8672 for more information

Once known as Pulau Blakang Mati or 'The Island Behind which Lies Death', **Sentosa** has served as a 19th-century refuge of pirates, a British military garrison and, after independence, a detention centre for citizens arrested under the Internal Security Act. It was at one time an eerie sort of place and an excellent setting for ghost stories. In 1972, the government turned the island into a theme park and resort area, with the new name Sentosa – meaning 'Isle of Peace and Tranquillity' in Malay – resulting from a name-the-island contest.

Interestingly, the name of the island is a misnomer. Far from invoking a sense of peace and contemplation, Sentosa is an activity-filled resort island. While some welcome the games arcade sort of atmosphere that prevails on the island, others have criticised Sentosa's lack of focus and its too numerous rides, displays and entertainment venues. The trick in 'doing' Sentosa is to choose the right attractions to visit – which can make the difference between a great day out and a disappointing one. But plans are already underway to finetune Sentosa's attractions: a whopping S$8-billion development programme (to be completed in 2010) will revitalise some of the island's more faded attractions.

Despite the emphasis on activity, there are still pockets of tranquillity that lend some credence to the Sentosa name. The armoury and tunnels at **Fort Siloso**, at the western tip of the island, are still on display, poignant reminders

Left: Shangri-La's Rasa Sentosa Hotel
Right: entrance to Sentosa

of the island's history. During World War II, the British had all their guns and cannon at the fort here pointing out to sea, expecting the Japanese to mount a frontal attack. The wily Japanese, however, attacked by land via Malaya from the north.

Golf enthusiasts might be content to head straight for the two 18-hole courses of the **Sentosa Golf Club** (tel: 6275 0022), while younger visitors may enjoy **Cinemania** (daily 11am–8pm; admission fee) or the **Trapeze** (Tues–Fri 4–6pm, Sat, Sun and public holidays 4–7pm; admission fee). Cinemania offers white-knuckled rides on computer-synchronised seats that claim to simulate roller coaster rides and speed races, while the Trapeze allows one to 'fly' across the trapeze like a circus performer – under the supervision of an instructor.

Wax Figures and Bird's Eye Views

The shuttle bus provided by **The Sentosa Resort & Spa** (tel: 6275 0331; www.thesentosa.com) takes you across the island's 1-km (½-mile) flower-lined causeway to the hotel. Make your way to one of the outdoor tables of **The Terrace** for breakfast. You may also wish to make an afternoon appointment at the hotel's **Spa Botanica** (tel: 6371 1318; www.spabotanica.com), which offers every conceivable treatment, from scrubs, massages and herbal wraps, to soothe aching bodies and tired minds.

After breakfast, take the Yellow Line Sentosa Bus to the Cable Car Plaza. For a quick history of Singapore, visit **Images of Singapore** (daily 9am–7pm; admission fee), located south of the Cable Car Plaza. Housed in a former military hospital, this wax museum has various exhibits that recount the social history and cultural diversity of Singapore.

Nearby is the **Carlsberg Sky Tower** (daily 9am–9pm; admission fee) – the tallest observatory tower in Asia at 135m (360ft) above sea level. Only worth doing on a clear day, it gives a bird's eye view of the Singapore skyline and the neighbouring southern islands. Alternatively, make your way to the **Flower Terrace** where the 37-m (120-ft) tall **Merlion** (daily 10am–8pm; admission fee) stands, a rather kitschy half-fish half-lion symbol of Singapore; an observatory at the top has nice views of the surroundings. Facing the Merlion is the colourful tilework of the **Merlion Walk**; by its side is the small **Herb and Spice Garden**, which features more than 250 types of spice and herb plants.

When you're done, walk towards **Sunset Bay** at **Siloso Beach**, and take the Beach Train to **Palawan Beach**. Here, a suspension bridge links the main island to a tiny islet billed as the southernmost point of the Asian continent. Two towers, clad in wood and bamboo, give you an elevated view out over the water, and you can catch a salty sea breeze here, even on the most sultry days.

Dolphins and Dragons

At Palawan Beach, take your pick from several options for a casual lunch, from the **Koufu Food Court**, which offers a wide range of local fare, to **Bora Bora Beach Bar**, a relaxing spot serving seafood and pasta. When you've had your fill, walk over to **Dolphin Lagoon** (daily 10.30am–6pm; admission fee includes entry to Underwater World), where rare pink dolphins endear themselves to visitors with their tail-flapping antics in the 'Meet the Dolphin' shows (11am, 1.30, 3.30 and 5.30pm). Afterwards, take the Red Line Sentosa Bus to **Underwater World** (daily 9am–9pm), home to more than 2,500 fish. Stroll through the clear acrylic tunnel and enjoy an unrestricted view of countless marine creatures, including stingrays, reef sharks, turtles and reef fish.

You now have the option of making a detour to the aforementioned **Fort Siloso** (daily 10am–6pm; admission fee), where guns, cannons and tunnels from World War II are combined with creative interactive displays to tell the history of Singapore's war-time past. The **Surrender Chambers** at the fort brings to life Singapore's formal surrender to the Japanese in 1942 through a gripping mix of real audio-visual footage, artefacts and realistic wax figurines. Otherwise, take the Green Line bus to the Cable Car Plaza, and stroll through the winding trails of the **Nature Walk/Dragon Trail** for a 1.5-km (1-mile) display of tropical flora and fauna.

If you're hungry, take the Green or Blue Line Sentosa Bus to the Ferry Terminal for an informal meal of local food at the **Asian Food Lover's Place**. If you are not too tired, make the **Musical Fountain** nearby your final stop. The half-hour 'Magical Sentosa' display (7.40 and 8.40pm nightly; free) will enthrall you with its leaping jets of water and laser lights interacting with a live actor on stage. And from here, a short bus ride will get you back to the mainland. A more scenic alternative is the cable car ride – enjoy the panoramic views as it crosses the sea to the HarbourFront Tower 2.

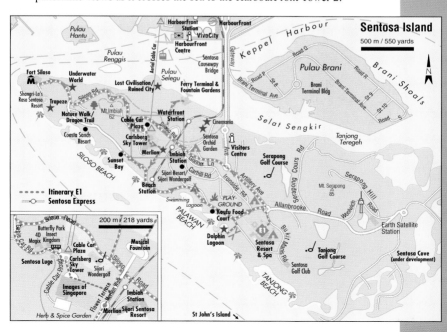

2. PULAU UBIN *(see pullout map)*

One of the last unspoilt areas left in Singapore, where village life is still a reality. Some 100 inhabitants still eke out a rustic living here by taking advantage of the island's natural resources, but this idyllic environment is under threat as development creeps in. A day trip or overnight.

Take a taxi to Changi Village Road or catch SBS bus 2 from Tanah Merah MRT Station, or bus 29 from Tampines MRT Station to Changi Village Bus Terminal. Go down Lorong Bekukong to Changi Point Ferry Terminal and board the ferry. The boatman will collect the S$2 fare for the 10-minute trip when he is ready to go. A full day is adequate for a quick look around; an overnight stay is great for unwinding into an earlier era, and waking to the sound of crowing roosters

Part of the appeal of **Pulau Ubin**, or Granite Island (www.nparks.gov.sg), a tiny island just off northeastern Singapore, is the contrast that it offers to the rest of efficient, urban Singapore. This begins with the ferry, which does not run to a schedule but departs when there are 12 passengers. The wait could vary from 5 to 20 minutes. The bumboats operate as early as 6am and the last one leaves Ubin island at about 10pm.

Getting your Bearings

On Pulau Ubin, orientate yourself at the **Information Kiosk** (daily 8.30am–5pm; tel: 6542 4108) just to the right of the jetty and get a map of the island. Then continue in the same direction towards the police post. Turn left and just behind the police post, you will find the **Sensory Trail**, which serves as an excellent introduction to the rustic and natural character of the island. Taking about 1½ hours to complete, the trail will guide you to feel the texture of lichen and banana bark as you walk among overhanging tendrils of aerial roots. Changes underfoot appeal to another set of senses and

understanding of the landscape. You will be able to touch, see and smell fruit trees, spices and herbs used in cooking and medicinal plants, as well as native plants of the mangrove forest. The signage is in braille as well as text. It is not a large area but it rewards leisurely exploration.

Rustic Sights

Make your way back to the jetty and head in the opposite direction, walking through the village centre where you can hire a bicycle for the day at very reasonable rates. Then take the road heading northeast to **Kampong Melayu**. It is about 3km (1¾ miles) and the last part of the route is a rough earth track. According to oral tradition, the village was pioneered by Endut Senin around the mid-1800s. This old Malay village is the last of its kind in Singapore and offers a glimpse into a simpler past lived close to the earth. While most villagers are friendly and hospitable, visitors to the area should respect their privacy.

Along the way, old rubber plantations and coconut groves hint at the island's agricultural past, while the secondary forest blooms with pale wild orchids and vivid orange nipah flowers. There are also fruit trees: yellow jackfruit, pungent *durian* and scarlet *rambutan* in season.

There is also a wide variety of fauna for nature lovers to enjoy. Brahminy kites and white-bellied fish eagles are fairly common and easy to spot as they soar on the rising air currents along the foreshore, while the diversity of insect life among the abundant flora also attracts woodpeckers and colourful bee-eaters with long beaks. Long-tailed macaque monkeys screech and swing overhead while colourful butterflies flit by in the foliage below. For a taste of mangrove terrain visit the swampy areas – easily accessible by paved roads – in the middle of the island.

Another excellent spot to enjoy Pulau Ubin's diverse nature offerings is **Chek Jawa** on the island's southeastern tip. The intertidal mudflats here are so fertile that they have engendered a stunningly rich ecosystem found nowhere else in Singapore. To protect Chek Jawa's flora and fauna, access is limited, and all visitors must book in advance to join the 45-minute guided tours scheduled on certain dates (tel: 6542 4108).

If you wish to stay the night, **Marina Country Club Ubin Resort** (tel: 6388 8388; www.marinacountryclub.com.sg) has basic cottage-style chalets for rent. Alternatively, camping is allowed on **Noordin Beach** and **Mamam Beach** on the northern coast; no visitor's permit is required.

To round off a day trip, head back to the village to return your bike and stop at one of the simple seafood eateries there for a drink and a plate of noodles before heading back to take the next ferry that leaves the island.

Left: getting to grips with nature on Pulau Ubin
Above: a Brahminy Kite swoops in for the kill at Pulau Ubin

3. MALACCA *(see map, p65)*

Head across the Causeway to the historic Malaysian town of Malacca. Just 260km (162 miles) away, Malacca was once the centre of a 15th-century trading empire and its glorious past is still evident today in its Dutch and Peranakan architecture. It's an easy one-day excursion, but staying overnight would allow more leisurely enjoyment of the sights.

Many tour agencies offer package tours to Malacca from Singapore (Farmosa, tel: 6534 1133 and Grassland Express, tel: 6293 1166 are recommended). If winging it on your own, take an air-conditioned coach (Malacca–Singapore Express, tel: 6293 5915) from the Kallang Bahru Terminal on Lavender Street. The fare (one-way) is S$11 for the journey, and buses leave at 8, 9, 10 and 11am, with another three departures at 2, 4 and 5pm. Bring your passport along and Malaysian currency for expenses

The bus takes you on the 260-km (162-mile) journey across the Singapore border to Malacca (Melaka) in about 5 hours. On arrival, take a taxi to one of the many hotels on Jalan Bendahara. As the taxis are not metered, the price should be settled at the start (about Ringgit Malaysia or RM10 to Jalan Bendahara). Accommodation ranges from the expensive: Renaissance Melaka (tel: 06-284 8888; www.marriott.com) and Hotel Equatorial (tel: 06-282 8333; www.equatorial.com), to the moderate: Hotel Puri (tel: 06-282 5588; hotelpuri.com) and Hotel Orkid (tel: 06-282 5555), all within 5 minutes of each other. Do ask about special offers, which can bring rates down by more than half.

A Famous Port

Malacca is where the history of Malaysia (formerly Malaya) began. In its heyday in the 1400s, traders from all over the world – including Persians, Arabs, Tamils, Javanese, Sundanese, Chinese, Thais and Burmese – descended on Malacca in search of profit through trade, piracy or plunder. Each in turn left something of their culture behind. The Chinese merchants who married local Malay women laid down the roots for the Peranakan community. Known as *baba* (men) and *nyonya* (women), the Peranakan accepted the practical realities of living in a Malay society by adopting the Malay dress and language, while at the same time continued upholding the social and religious norms of their forefathers in Fujian, China.

By the end of the 15th century, Malacca had become the centre of a great trading empire and held an undisputed claim over the whole of the southern Malay peninsula. However, Malacca's golden age came to an end in 1511 when it fell to the Portuguese, who ruled for more than 100 years, before they were ousted by the Dutch, who in turn ceded Malacca to the British in 1795. As a result, the stamp of Malacca's colonial forefathers is found everywhere in the city; most evidently in the architecture but also among the community of Portuguese Eurasians – descendants of intermarriage between Portuguese sailors and local

Left: a 19th-century portrait of a Malaccan *baba*
Right top: Peranakan silver belt buckle from Jonker Street

excursions

women in the 16th century. A small Eurasian enclave is still found in Malacca today, in the Portuguese Settlement some 3km (1¼ miles) from the city centre. Some of the older folk still speak Cristao, a medieval dialect of southeastern Portugal that is spoken nowhere else in the world today.

Have your first Peranakan meal at the **Bulldog Café** (145 Jalan Bendahara), where the speciality is *popiah*, a lip-smacking paper-thin roll filled with shredded bamboo shoot and radish. The old-style corner shop, **Restoran Lee** (155 Jalan Bendahara), is open late into the night for locals who like to linger over a satisfying seafood meal. Have a simple dish of noodles with seafood, or splurge on steamed Sri Lankan crabs. A young coconut makes a refreshing drink and dessert all in one. For more food options, check www.visitormalaysia.com/foodnbeverage_malacca.htm.

Historical Centre

Next morning, leave your overnight bag with the porter and go down Jalan Bendahara towards the town centre. Depending on where you are staying, either walk or take a *becak* (trishaw) to one of the most photographed sights in Malacca – **A Famosa**, also known as Porta de Santiago. Built as a fortress by the Portuguese in 1511, it once enclosed a castle, two palaces, a government hall and five churches. The fort repelled numerous attacks for 150 years before succumbing to the Dutch in 1641 after an eight-month siege. The Dutch repaired the fort only to have it blown to pieces by the British some 150 years later. What remains today are the ruins of a stone gateway, saved from destruction by Singapore's founder, Sir Stamford Raffles, in 1808.

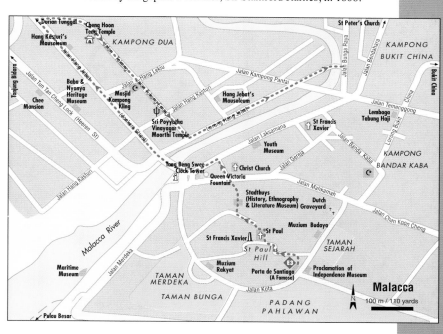

Take the winding steps up **St Paul's Hill** where looming overhead are yet more ruins – the remains of **St Paul's Church**. It was erected by the Portuguese in 1521 and later used by the Jesuit missionaries. St Francis Xavier was enshrined here temporarily in 1552 and the Dutch later used St Paul's as burial grounds – seen today in the numerous tombstones that line the inside of the church ruins.

Take the winding stairs west of St Paul's which lead downhill and then turn right at the first intersection. Soon you will see the maroon-coloured walls of the **Stadthuys** on your right, former offices of the Dutch governors and now the **History, Ethnography & Literature Museum** (Tues–Sun 9am–6pm; admission fee). Immediately past the museum entrance, the original drainage system of Dutch laterite blocks is displayed. Porcelain, currency and weaponry collections and a Dutch house are also on display. There is a model of the city in the history galleries upstairs, which look out over the city centre.

A Cool Respite

More rewarding is the **Literature Museum**, accessible via a charming courtyard, which shows the history of Malacca in words and pictures. There is an excellent explanation of the structure of Malaccan society and a summary of the exploits of the legendary hero Hang Tuah. It is also one of the few exhibition halls which are air-conditioned so you might want to linger here while contemplating the fact that the Stadthuys, built in 1650, is the oldest known Dutch building still standing in Asia.

Exit the museum and take the stairs down on your right where you will see a clocktower and an open area, sometimes referred to as the **Red Square**. The lovely fountain nearby was built to commemorate the Diamond Jubilee of Queen Victoria. Immediately to the right is the massive **Christ Church**, built with brick shipped from Holland in 1753, and supported by beams, each hewn from a single tree. Unfortunately, the church is not opened to visitors.

Antique Hunt

Cross the square and go over the bridge across the river to the **Jonker Street** antique area. Turn left and, at Hereen House, turn into **Jalan Tan Cheng Lock**, which is full of galleries and craft shops. At No 48–50 on your right, ring the bell for admittance into the **Baba Nyonya Heritage Museum** (daily 10am–12.30pm and 2–4.30pm; admission fee; tel: 06-283 1273). This is a private house – or rather a residence made up of three houses belonging to a wealthy Peranakan family – open for public viewing on half-hour guided tours. The décor, household effects and the guide's narrative all give insights into this unique hybrid culture.

After your tour, carry on to the **Melaqa House** at No 70. Walk through this typical Peranakan house – much larger than it appears to be from the outside – with its double air-wells and pick up a souvenir from its extensive arts and crafts collection. To complete the experience, proceed to the **Restoran Peranakan Town House** at No 107 (tel: 06-284 5001) for lunch.

At the end of Jalan Tan Cheng Lock, make a sharp right into Jalan Tokong, where the ornate **Cheng Hoon Teng Temple** stands with characters from Chinese myth and legend sculpted onto the roof. This is the oldest Chinese temple in the country, built in 1645 with materials shipped from China – a tradition which continues into this century – with China-made roof tiles used in the recent 2000 renovations. At an angle across the street is the impressive hall of the **Malaysia Buddhist Association**. Further along the street are shops selling joss sticks, incense, oils and materials for worship, as well as paper models of houses, cars and the other good things in life, to burn as offerings for ancestors who have gone to the next world.

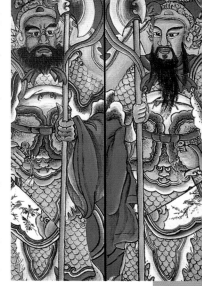

Continue walking to Jalan Tukang Emas, to **Kampung Kling Mosque**, again one of the oldest in the country, with its three-tiered roof, Sumatran influences and a Moorish style minaret. In the courtyard, its restoration in 1999 is documented. Almost immediately next to it is the **Sri Poyyatha Vinayagar Moorthi Temple**, built on land allocated by the Dutch rulers, and dedicated to the elephant-headed god, Ganesh, known for his power as a remover of obstacles.

Turn right at Jalan Hang Kasturi and make your way back to the town centre by **Jalan Hang Jebat**, a favourite haunt of antique seekers in the Jonker Street area. Back at the town centre, if time and energy permit, proceed to Jalan Laksamana for a quick look at the **Maritime Museum** (daily 9am–5pm; admission fee; tel: 06 283 6538) and the replica Portuguese ship *Fior de la Mar*.

Head back towards your hotel on the less touristy **Jalan Bunga Raya**. Shops here serve the local population, and there are good bargains, especially

Left: what's left of the Portuguese: the A Famosa Fort
Right: Chinese gods painted on doors to guard the house

in the row of fabric shops towards the end of the street. Pop into the department store, **Madam King's**, at No 126, for an idea of local prices and the lifestyles of ordinary Malaccans.

When you're ready to return to Singapore, head towards the river on Jalan Munshi Abdullah, cross the overhead pedestrian bridge and you're in the mêlée of the bus terminal. The Singapore–Malacca ticket counter is to the right. Or just ask; people are friendly here. Have a cup of the excellent local coffee while waiting for your bus.

4. BINTAN ISLAND *(see map, p69)*

One of the 3,000 islands belonging to Indonesia's Riau Archipelago, Bintan Island offers a range of luxury seaside resorts perfect for a quick overnight getaway from the urban pressures of Singapore.

High-speed catamarans make the 45-minute trip from Singapore's Tanah Merah Ferry Terminal (TMFT) to Bintan's Bandar Bentan Telani (BBT) ferry terminal, on the north shore of the island. Allow 30–40 minutes to get to TFMT by taxi from the city centre. All resorts provide transfers from the BBT upon arrival. Book ferry tickets with Bintan Resort Ferries (tel: 6542 4369). For accommodation, check www.bintan-resorts.com. Alternatively, book a package with BRF Holidays (tel: 6293 3191; www.brfholidays.com.sg). Don't forget your passport

Pulau Bintan, or 'Star Island', nearly three times the size of Singapore at 1,030sq km (398sq miles) is the largest island in the Riau archipelago, which is part of Sumatra, Indonesia. Most of the island is made up of thick jungle, swamp and mountains with isolated pockets of people living in villages. However, in the last few years, some parts of the sleepy island have been turned into industrial zones while on the northern shore, the stretch of powder white **Pasir Panjang** beach has been developed into a mega resort area with a string of hotels, golf courses and other tourist facilities.

Your choice of resort will depend on the nature of your preferred activity. Serenity is the keynote of the upscale **Banyan Tree Bintan** (tel: 6849 5800) which hugs a cliff at one of the beach. It has a first rate spa, and villas with either a private pool or deck jacuzzi overlooking the South China Sea. The villas are ingeniously built into the sprawling rainforest landscape and connected by narrow winding paths to the reception area and restaurants. If you can't be bothered to walk, buggys are also available to ferry you from one place to another. You can enjoy your stay in complete calm and seclusion, or follow a well-marked nature trail for leisurely exercise.

Left: fisherman mending nets
Right top: Angsana Resort's inviting pool

More Resort Options

For organised activity and lavish meals there is **Club Med Ria Bintan** (tel: 1800-258 2633) with its French-style beach culture atmosphere. At the stylish Mediterranean-inspired **Nirwana Gardens Resort** (tel: 6213 5830), the accent is on family fun. The bonus of staying here is the proximity of the picturesque **Kelong Restaurant** with its fresh seafood meals, situated just next door. For laid-back chalet-style accommodation, there is the **Mayang Sari Beach Resort** (tel: 6213 5830). This resort is adjacent to the popular **Asmara Tropical Spas** (www.asmaraspas.com), which is convenient if you wish to indulge in a spa treatment.

Nearby, the **Mana Mana Beach Club** (tel: 6339 8878) offers a wide range of watersports facilities as well as accommodation. Golfers tend to gravitate towards **Bintan Lagoon** (tel: 6223 3223) with two 18-hole golf courses designed by Jack Nicklaus and Ian Baker-Finch.

New on the scene is the **Angsana Resort and Spa** (tel: 6849 5788), located just next door to the Banyan Tree. Angsana offers spa treatments and massages in open-air pavilions facing the sea, which are simply heavenly. Book spa treatments early, even before leaving Singapore, as almost everyone who stays here gravitates to the spa at some point of their stay. Try and pick a weekday: room and ferry rates are cheaper, and your hotel is also less likely to be overrun by hordes of holiday-makers from Singapore.

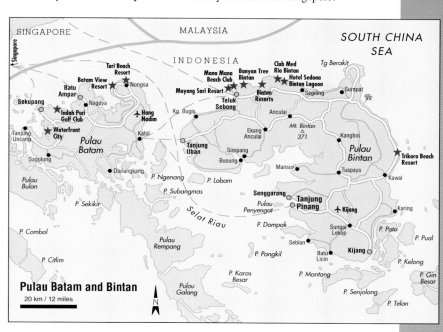

Pulau Batam and Bintan
20 km / 12 miles

Day Trips

For a complete change of pace, you might consider a day trip to bustling **Tanjung Pinang** on the southwestern coast, the island's most important urban area, and the ancient capital of the Riau province. Filled with traces of Malay, Chinese and Dutch influences, this town is a huddle of wooden houses on stilts, flanking a series of wooden parallel *pelantar* (walkways) that jut out to sea.

Seemingly endless cavalcades of motorcycles jostle pedestrians and other vehicles along the crowded streets, dotted with vendors selling tapioca and banana chips from mobile stands. Visit the market at **Jalan Pasar Ikan** where mounds of fruit, vegetables, herbs and spices are displayed, together with bags of sliced, dried seafood pastes that are fried to make a popular snack of crisp, light crackers called *keropok*.

For respite from the clamour, walk into the oasis of calm offered by the **Vihara Dharma Sasana Buddhist Temple**, complete with dancing dragons on the rooftop, on Jalan Merdeka, close to the waterfront. Or take a boat to the little island of **Penyengat** just across the Tanjung Pinang harbour, to visit the cradle of Malay civilisation. The first book on Malay grammar was published here in 1857, laying the foundation for Bahasa Indonesia, the official *lingua franca* of the sprawling Indonesian islands that surround Singapore on three sides. Village life is preserved here and the more than 2,000 people live and go about mending nets, fixing boats, and harvesting papayas and coconuts. Some major sights include the **Sultan's Mosque** and the **Royal Graveyard**, both decorated in distinctive warm yellow colours, bringing to mind the gold associated with royalty. On a hill overlooking the town is the restored **Bukit Kursi Fort**, one of the three forts built in the 19th century as a defence against the Dutch.

Most resorts should be able to organise a day trip, but if you are interested in something a little different, BRF Holidays organises eco and heritage tours, adventure trekking and traditional fishing trips. Tanjung Pinang can also be accessed directly from Singapore's Tanah Merah Ferry Terminal.

Above: royal graveyard, Penyengat
Right: hanging out fishing nets to dry

Leisure Activities

SHOPPING

From Orchard Road's shiny new shopping centres to the charming shophouses of Chinatown, Little India and Arab Street, there is a wide selection of shopping places to satisfy most shopaholics. In a country where shopping is a national pastime, shops are generally open daily from 10–11am to about 9pm, so you can literally shop till you drop. Bargain only in the smaller shops and let the salesperson know if you intend to pay by credit card, as this form of payment sometimes carries a 2–4 percent surcharge which has to be factored into the price.

There is a 5 percent Goods and Services Tax (GST) on most purchases in Singapore, which tourists can refund for purchases above S$100 *(see page 91).*

There are no distinct sales periods that follow the seasons. Stores mark down their prices periodically. The best time to shop is from late May to early July during the annual Great Singapore Sale. Post Christmas and Chinese New Year are also good for bargains.

The Singapore Tourism Board (STB) has authorised selected shops to display its Singapore Gold Circle's Promise of Excellence sticker as a symbol of its recommendation. If you meet with less than satisfactory retailer practices, bring your grievances to **STB** (tel: 1800 736 2000), the **Retail Promotion Centre** (tel: 6352 9909), or the **Consumers' Association of Singapore** (CASE, tel: 6463 1811). Alternatively, go to the **Small Claims Tribunal** (tel: 6435 5937) for fast-track legal help or visit the Subordinate Courts' **E@DR Centre** (www.e-adr.org.sg) for dispute resolution via email.

What to Buy

With the increasing affluence of its people and a relatively strong Singapore dollar, the island state's identity as a shopping paradise has seen a gradual change from a centre for bargain buys to upmarket goods.

Left: handicrafts on Arab Street
Right: fashion boutiques abound

Cameras and Audio Equipment

Prices are attractive, particularly for photographic equipment and the latest portable CD or MP3 player. CDs and MP3s are often much cheaper here than elsewhere too. It's a good idea to get an international guarantee, but if you want to take a risk on imported goods intended only for the local market, you can save on the price.

Computer Equipment

Being such a wired country, Singapore is a good place to purchase both hardware and software, both locally made and imported. Apple computers are locally assembled in Singapore. Don't forget to check the voltage on the equipment you buy. The law comes down hard on bootleg software and frequent raids are carried out at shopping malls specialising in computers – so buy the genuine stuff and ask for a guarantee.

Watches and Jewellery

Watches are sold tax-free, and the choice is endless, from a lifetime's investment in a Rolex to a fun Swatch. Gold jewellery is also a good buy. While the older generation prefers ornaments crafted in 22K yellow gold – available at jewellers in Serangoon Road and Chinatown – the younger set tends to go for 18K white or yellow gold with precious or semi-precious stones. Contemporary jewellery designs from several local chains like **Gold Heart** and **Lee Hwa** are found in many shopping centres, and of course, major names in jewellery are all here: **Tiffany, Cartier** and **Bvlgari** amongst them.

Live orchid blooms – sold under the

Risis brand – plated with 22K gold to preserve their beauty can be worn as rings, earrings, pendants or bracelets. Mikimoto pearls from Japan, fashionable black pearls from the South Pacific and freshwater pearls of all colours are available.

Fashion and Accessories

Designer shops and boutiques abound in the big Orchard Road malls. Giving international brand names a run for their money are local ones such as **Song+Kelly21** (Level 2, Isetan Orchard at Wisma Atria), **Celia Loe** (02-21 Raffles City) and **Daniel Yam** (01-141 Suntec City Mall). Other local names of note include **projectshopBLOODbros** (01-16 Wisma Atria), **M)Phosis** (B1-52 Ngee Ann City) and **Bodynits** (02-182 Marina Square). Or you can choose to have that special dress copied, or a suit made-to-measure by a tailor. The **Far East Shopping Centre** has a wide variety of tailors to meet your needs. Remember to be specific in your design and insist on more than one fitting. For something more Asian, there is imported batik from Malaysia and Indonesia as well as Singapore-made contemporary batik from **Blue Ginger** (02-03 Raffles Hotel Shopping Arcade). You can also find silk fabrics from China, Thailand, India and Malaysia.

There's a whole range of shoes, from Bally to the local **Charles & Keith** and a large range of sports shoes. Also available in the

shops are bags of all kinds, from delicate evening clutches to heavy-duty cabin trunks.

Antiques and Asian Handicrafts

The selection of antiques and handicrafts from Bangkok to Borneo and beyond is comprehensive. You can find baskets and shell work from the Philippines; lacquerware and delicate porcelain from Japan; figurines from Burma and Thailand; Indian *papier mâché* and brassware; and cloisonnéware and ceramics from China. If you can't carry it all, then ship it back home in a Korean camphorwood chest. Prints and maps as well as old editions of books on the region can be found, and also old porcelain, figurines and coins. Insist on a certificate of antiquity for a genuine antique purchase. Try **Tanglin Shopping Centre** for antiques and **Dempsey Road** near the Botanic Gardens for Asian handicrafts and furnishings.

Oriental Carpets

You will find an enormous selection of beautiful Oriental carpets, from tribal rugs to exquisite silk carpets in glorious colours and intricate designs. When buying, look at the workmanship: the dyeing, knotting and clipping in the finished carpet are important criteria. The more knots per square centimetre, the finer (and more expensive) the carpet, so turn it over and have a look at the back. Be sure also to take the carpet into daylight to see the colours. **Tanglin Shopping Centre** has several good carpet stores.

Where to Buy
Arab Street

In **Arab Street**, just off Beach Road, a distinctly Malay atmosphere lingers. It is *the* place to shop for handwoven baskets, batik and all things Islamic. Shops are piled high with leather bags, baskets and rattan goods, purses and shoes while bright trinkets glitter invitingly. *(see also Itinerary 5, page 40)*

Little India

Singapore's Little India, Serangoon Road and the neighbouring side streets are the place for anything from spices and jewellery to Indian silk from the subcontinent. **Mustafa Centre** (tel: 6295 5855) at Syed Alwi Road is a large 24-hour shopping mall popular for

Left: batik galore at Arab Street

shopping guide

its low-priced electronic goods among other bargains like garments and knick-knacks. **Little India Arcade**, at the corner of Serangoon and Hastings roads, is a series of colourful restored shophouses stuffed with interesting Indian paraphernalia.

A stone's throw from Little India is **Parco Bugis Junction**, a multi-level shopping mall linked underground to the Bugis MRT Station. Apart from the Japanese **Seiyu** department store, there are scores of retail outlets.

Chinatown

Chinatown is the place to go to for things Chinese; wander the tiny shops of **Pagoda Street** and **Temple Street** and browse the stalls at the **Chinatown Night Market** to purchase collectibles such as Chinese teapots, fans, embroidered silk shirts, or Chinese herbs such as ginseng. At **People's Park Complex** along Eu Tong Sen Street you can find all kinds of fabrics, while the more upmarket **Yue Hwa** department store (tel: 6538 9233) next door allows you to shop for exquisite Chinese clothing and handicrafts in air-conditioned comfort. **Chinatown Point** opposite is a haven for Chinese arts and crafts and also electronic goods, cameras and watches.

Holland Village

Holland Shopping Centre in Holland Village, a little further out of town, is the expat haunt, and you'll find a wide range of bags, shoes, jewellery and clothes from batik to comfortable casuals. An especially good place to solve all your gift and souvenir headaches is **Lim's Arts and Crafts** (tel: 6467 1300) on the second floor of the mall.

North Bridge Road

Funan Centre at North Bridge Road has been renamed **Funan the IT Mall** in deference to its huge array of computer equipment and software. On the ground floor there is always a computer fair of some sort where bargains are to be found. Also at North Bridge Road are **Peninsula Plaza**, **Peninsula Shopping Centre** and the **Adelphi**, with numerous shops specialising in cameras and audio equipment. Closer to the City Hall MRT Station is **Raffles City**, a six-storey mall with a wide array of retail outlets and several good eateries. Just opposite facing Beach Road is the **Raffles Hotel Shopping Arcade** with a number of designer boutiques, antique shops, a Tiffany jewellery store and a gift shop selling Raffles Hotel memorabilia.

Marina Square/Suntec City

Marina Square is an extensive mall that houses a bowling alley and is conveniently linked to a cineplex. There are also many boutiques and shoe shops and a handful of eating places. A raised walkway takes you to **Millenia Walk**, with its more upmarket shops and cafés. Connected by an underpass is the mega-sized **Suntec City Mall**. This mall has countless shops selling clothes,

Above: shopping in Chinatown

shoes, bags, electronic equipment, books and sports apparel, a huge French Carrefour supermarket plus numerous restaurants.

Joining this shopping enclave is a subterranean shopping mall called **CityLink Mall**. Its 5,600sq m (60,000sq ft) of retail space, with stores like MPH books and HMV records, conveniently connects City Hall MRT Station underground to Marina Square, Suntec Mall and the new **Esplanade Mall** adjoining the Esplanade – Theatres on the Bay.

Tanglin, Orchard and Scotts roads
Orchard Road is to Singapore what Fifth Avenue is to New York and the Champs-Elysees to Paris. Even people who have never been to Singapore have heard of Orchard Road – such is its claim to shopping fame (for a complete summary see *Itinerary 2*, *page 28*). **Tanglin Mall**, at the junction of Grange and Tanglin roads, heralds the start of this shopping precinct. From this point onwards is a shopaholic's dream come true – one dazzling mall after the other filled with

swanky department stores and any number of retail outlets and designer brand boutiques. There are malls dedicated to pleasing young children (**Forum The Shopping Mall**), spotty adolescents (**Pacific Plaza** and the **Heeren**), brides-to-be (**Delfi Orchard**), antique and carpet collectors (**Tanglin Shopping Centre**), camera buffs (**Lucky Plaza**), as well as the well-heeled (**Hilton Gallery**, **Palais Renaissance** and the **Paragon**) along with the usual shopping centres crammed with clothing, shoes, accessories, jewellery and household goods ad infinitum.

Not everyone is clear where Tanglin Road merges into Orchard Road (it is the junction where the Orchard Parade Hotel is found by the way) but one sure sign is the intensity in the number of shopping malls. There is a respite – and the men will thank the city planners for this – at the top end of Orchard Road just after the Le Meridien Hotel until the shopping monster rears its head in the form of **Plaza Singapura** just past the Istana presidential palace. Mercifully, Orchard Road is dotted with sidewalk cafés and stylish coffee shops where you can rest your feet, sip on an ice-cold coffee and watch shoppers heave their heavy bags.

Suburban Areas
Apart from **Holland Village** (see *page 75*), the suburbs are where some of the best bargains are to be found. Many are accessible by MRT; like **Tampines** (Century Square and Tampines Mall); **Bishan** (Junction 8); **Jurong** (Jurong Point and IMM); **Yishun** (Northpoint); **Choa Chu Kang** (Lot 1); and **Woodlands** (Causeway Point).

EATING OUT

Eating is a great passion in Singapore – it is possible to eat out at every meal 365 days of the year and not go back to the same place twice. At the many food courts sprinkled all over the island, you can sample different cuisines in a single venue cooked fresh by an array of vendors – ideal for a quick and informal meal. Alternatively, there is a staggering choice of restaurants where the traditional cuisines of the main ethnic groups are further subdivided into regional specialities.

Many Asian styles are represented: fiery South Indian curries served on banana leaf as well as *tandoor* grills and *naan* breads of North India. Delicate Cantonese, refined Teochew, robust Hunanese and sumptuous Beijing dishes are some of the Chinese regional cuisines found at restaurants. Of course, the spices of Malay and Indonesian *nasi padang*, the fresh herbs that characterise the flavours of Indochina, and the complex flavours of Thai cooking, can all be sampled, plus the whole range of Japanese cuisine from cold-weather stews to elegant *sashimi* – and puffer fish for the adventurous.

There is also excellent Western food in Singapore, particularly French and Italian, with wines to match, albeit at a price; and of course American ribs, burgers and steaks. In this environment, as you might expect, masters of fusion cuisine are inspired to high levels of creativity, blending seemingly disparate ingredients with flair.

One unique style of cooking deserves special mention: Peranakan food originated from the blending of Malay and Chinese cultures among the communities of the 19th-century Straits Settlements. Dishes often require long hours of slow cooking and complicated preparations; flavours are complex and can range from fiery to delicate. Desserts in the form of little cakes called *nyonya kueh* are colourful, often rich with coconut cream and sweetened with fragrant palm sugar.

In the vast array of dishes available, there are several which lie particularly close to Singaporean hearts: Hainanese chicken rice (slices of chicken with chicken-flavoured rice and chilli sauce), *satay* (barbecued meat on skewers) and chilli crab, which redefines 'finger licking good' as you mop up the chilli-tomato sauce with chunks of bread, preferably outdoors and within sight of the sea. Another favourite is fish head curry, in which a whole head, eyes and all looking back at you, is cooked in curry with eggplant, tomatoes and lady's fingers (okra).

All this delicious food needs something worthy to wash it down, and the locally brewed Tiger and Anchor beers are excellent choices. Or try Chinese tea, fresh lime and soya bean milk – all popular local tipples. Don't leave without tasting a Singapore Sling: a zesty blend of gin, cherry brandy, Cointreau, pineapple juice and fresh lime.

In the following pages, price categories for a three-course meal for two without drinks are as follows: $$$ = above S$80, $$ = S$50–80, $ = less than S$50.

Indonesian
Sanur
04-17 Centrepoint, Orchard Road
Tel: 6734 2192
Furnished in Asian dark wood and batik, the restaurant is very popular. The *gado gado* salad with potatoes, eggs and vegetables in peanut sauce is a light meal in itself. The spicy beef *rendang* and *tahu telur*, fried bean-curd with sweet soya sauce, are must-trys.$

Left: Centrepoint shopping mall in the heart of Orchard Road
Right: an array of Peranakan dishes

The Rice Table
43 Cuppage Road
Tel: 6735 9117, and
03-028 Suntec City Mall
Tel: 6333 0248
If you love Indonesian food and want to sample a little of everything, this is the place to satisfy your craving. This is one of the very few eateries in town serving Dutch-Indonesian *rijsttafel*; 14 dishes are served for lunch and a whopping 20 dishes for dinner. $

Malay

Hajjah Maimunah Restaurant
11 Jalan Pisang
Tel: 6291 3132
This functional self-service restaurant displays its dishes behind a glass-covered counter. Tell the server how many people are eating and indicate your selection. These will be dished up and then served at the table. Try *ikan bakar,* barbecued fish in sweet soya sauce, and the tender *rendang* (dry beef curry). $

Tepak Sireh Restoran
73 Sultan Gate
Tel: 6396 4373
This resplendent mustard-coloured building adjacent to the Istana Kampong Gelam was originally built for Malay royalty. Its recipes, reportedly handed down from generations, live up to expectations. Serves only buffet-style meals; recommended are its spicy and tender beef *rendang* (dry beef curry), squid curry (*gulai sotong*) and pandan tea. $

Thai

Thanying
Level 2 Amara Hotel
165 Tanjong Pagar Road
Tel: 6227 7856
Serves authentic royal Thai cuisine in gracious Thai style. The green curry is excellent, as are the stuffed chicken wings and minced shrimp grilled on a stick of sugar cane, especially eaten with olive rice. And be sure to leave room for the delicious desserts from the buffet. Pricey but worth every cent. $$$

Yhingthai Palace
01-04, 36 Purvis Street
Tel: 6337 1161
Located in one of Singapore's trendy food streets, this restaurant serves delightfully robust Thai cuisine. Must-trys include the squid salad, three-flavoured fried fish, string beans with shrimp, and for dessert, a perennial favourite – mango with sticky rice. Also owns Wang Yhingthai, along the same stretch, that caters to *halal* diners. $$

Cantonese

Chef Chan's Restaurant
01-02 Odeon Towers, 331 North Bridge Road
Tel: 6250 3363
Unconventional black walls, chefs clad in black jackets, and huge Chinese lanterns imported from Guangzhou – as well as Chef Chan's personal collection of Chinese antiques – is the setting for the innovative Cantonese

Above: eating out – Singapore style

cuisine here. Signature dishes are crispy roast chicken, black-pepper beef tenderloin, and braised shark's fin with crab roe. $$–$$$

Golden Peony
Conrad Centennial Hotel
Temasek Boulevard
Tel: 6432 7482
Refined Cantonese cuisine in intimate and plush surroundings. Delicate *dim sum* is available at lunchtime. Round off the meal with some silky noodles with crabmeat in a rich broth, and fragrant Chinese tea served in individual lidded cups. At dinner time, classic dishes include minced pigeon served in lettuce cups, and *tang-ho* leaves cooked with century and salted eggs. $$$

Teahouse
3/F, China Square Food Centre
51 Telok Ayer Street
Tel: 6533 0660
Serves all-day Cantonese *dim sum* the old-fashioned way – on trolleys rolled before each guest. You will find the usual fare: fluffy steamed pork buns, sweet and savoury baked puff pastries, fried stuffed bean curd skins. For more heartier fare, try crab noodles, fried prawns with butter egg floss and curry, and silky fish maw soup. $–$$

Szechuan

Min Jiang
Goodwood Park Hotel, Scotts Road
Tel: 6737 5337
Traditional décor greets you at the entrance, with a red lacquer balustrade surrounding the exterior. Popular for business lunches and celebration dinners. Try the camphor-and-tea smoked duck, chicken with diced red chilli peppers and fried string beans as main courses, ending with the Szechuan pancake for dessert. The immaculate service never fails to impress. $$$

Indian

Annalakshmi
104 Amoy Street
Tel: 6339 9993
Exquisite setting to match the fine vegetarian fare. Traditional artwork displayed is on sale and food is prepared and served entirely by volunteers

of an Indian cultural association. There is a buffet at lunch and dinner, but this is worth forgoing to try the airy *thosai* pancakes made from rice flour and lentils. The menu has no prices and diners pay as much (or as little) as they wish – the money funds artistic and charitable activities. $

Kinara
57A Boat Quay
Tel: 6533 0412
Elegant traditional setting with contemporary touches. Elaborate wall friezes especially commissioned by Indian craftsmen artfully lit with minimalist fixtures. Delicately spiced North Indian dishes as well as grills from the *tandoor*, to be eaten with fluffy *naan* breads and saffron *basmati* rice. Skip the sinfully rich desserts, unless you need a sugar-induced high. $$

Madras New Woodlands
12–14 Upper Dickson Road
Tel: 6297 1594
Functional neighbourhood feel in this popular vegetarian restaurant. Try the set lunch complete with hot tamarind soup, rice and a dozen different dishes plus dessert. Also serves delicious *thosai* pancakes. $

Muthu's Curry
138 Race Course Road
Tel: 6392 1722
Recently renovated and sporting trendy minimalist decor, this 35-year-old restaurant serves a potent fish head curry – its award-winning speciality – as well as other delicious dishes such as mutton chops in tomato puree and spices, *masala* chicken and fish cutlet – all served on banana leaves instead of plates. Forget the cutlery and eat with your fingers. $–$$

Right: claypot chicken is a local favourite

Peranakan

House of Peranakan Cuisine
Meritus Negara Hotel, 10 Claymore Road
Tel: 6733 4411
One of the better Peranakan restaurants around. Specialities include chilli squid on hot plate, *ngor hiang* (Chinese stuffed rolls) and various clear soups and slow-cooked curries prepared the traditional way. The refreshing lime juice with bits of jelly is a must. $$

Indochinese

Indochine
49B Club Street
Tel: 6323 0503
An idyllic setting for dishes from the kitchens of Vietnam, Laos and Cambodia, – as interpreted by the chefs of Indochine. Lots of fresh green herbs go with fried meats, noodles in rich soups and melt-in-the-mouth fish baked in coconut custard. If the food does not impress, the artefacts on display certainly will. $$$

Seafood

Long Beach Seafood Restaurant
01-02 East Coast Seafood Centre
1202 East Coast Parkway
Tel: 6448 3636
Cheap and cheerful décor, with plastic table cloths and nice ambience thanks to its seafront location. Excellent chilli crab and black pepper crab. Fried baby squid is also popular, as is chicken stuffed with minced prawn. $$

Tung Lok Seafood Gallery
Block B, Level 2 East Coast Recreation Centre, East Coast Parkway
Tel: 6246 0555
This upmarket seafood restaurant is a place to linger over your meal compared to most slap-dash seafood eateries. Calming blue-green colours matched by attentive service

sets the mood. Apart from the usual dishes like chilli crab and fried squid, the restaurant prides itself on its inventive menu of dishes like lobsters in Chinese wine and prawns in wasabi-mayonnaise sauce. $$$

Snappers
Level 1 Ritz-Carlton Millenia
7 Raffles Avenue
Tel: 6434 5288
Western-style and fusion seafood-based cuisine in a hotel known for its high dining standards. Sophisticated setting opens out to the spectacular pool. Dishes like softshell crab in spicy mango sauce and *shoyu* cod with porcini mushrooms are surefire hits. Non-fish eaters are not ignored: there is a small selection of meat and chicken dishes. Leave room for its excellent desserts. $$$

Fusion

Club Chinois
02-18 Orchard Parade Hotel, 1 Tanglin Road
Tel: 6834 0660
A rare combination of elegance and informality, the restaurant is decorated with eclectic artwork from the owner's collection. Signature dishes include tender rack of lamb with five-spices and fried rice with a hint of salt-fish. Creative chef creates new menus constantly, so just let the *maitre'd* propose. There is *dim sum* for breakfast. The set menu at lunch offers excellent value. $$$

Coriander Leaf
02-03 Clarke Quay
Tel: 6732 3354
Atmospheric restaurant showcasing a brilliant pan-Asian menu given a Western spin. Try the mezze (various dips with grilled chicken wings and spinach triangles), spiced-rubbed rack of lamb, and for dessert, the orange-prune tart. Delicious sides include various *naan* breads and coriander-spiked rice. The menu changes seasonally. $$$

European

Ember
Hotel 1929, 50 Keong Saik Road
Tel: 6347 1928
Chef-owner Sebastien Ng is one of Singapore's most talented chefs. His Modern European cuisine is delightfully robust yet refined,

Left: delectable *dim sum*

and comes with wonderful Asian accents. A must-try is the slow-roasted lamb loin. $$–$$$

French

Au Jardin Les Amis

EJH Corner House, Singapore Botanic Gardens Visitor Centre, Cluny Road
Tel: 6466 8812

Contemporary French haute cuisine served in an elegant colonial house overlooking lush gardens. Prior booking for the fixed-priced *menu degustation* is de rigueur. Also has a sister restaurant called Les Amis at Shaw Centre in Orchard Road (tel: 6733 2225), which serves equally fine French fare in more contemporary suroundings. $$$

Saint Pierre

01-01 Central Mall, 3 Magazine Road
Tel: 6438 0887

With a half-dozen variety of foie gras on the menu, this restaurant is popular and reservations are a must. Saint Pierre is owned by Belgian native Emmanuel Stroobant. All-time favourites include pan-fried foie gras with caramelised green apple, braised black cod with white miso and shiraz sauce, and Grandma Stroobant's flourless chocolate cake with strawberry coulis. $$$

Italian

Buko Nero

126 Tanjong Pagar Road
Tel: 6324 6225

Forget about décor here. You are here to eat, not imbibe the Ikea-like environs. Run by an Italian-husband and Singaporean-wife couple, the menu reflects this Italian-Asian marriage. With a maximum capacity of 24 persons, book a table days ahead to sample innovative dishes like lemongrass marinated duck or its delicious *tofu* tower. $$

Da Paolo

80 Club Street
Tel: 6224 7081

Understated décor in white and wood sets the tone for sophistication without stuffiness. Excellent fresh pastas, including spaghetti *vongole* (fresh clams) and a rich squid ink pasta well worth getting your teeth coated with the black sauce. Save room for the excellent tiramisu. $$$

International

Bakerzin

02-09 Paragon, 290 Orchard Road
Tel: 6333 6647

Singapore's most famous dessert place offers a mouthwatering selection of dainty cakes. Its souffles are divine. Heartier meals – sandwiches, soups and salads – are also served. $

Crossroads Café

Marriott Hotel, 320 Orchard Road
Tel: 6831 4605

Perch yourself at this sidewalk café and watch all of Orchard Road pass by while you sample its varied and delicious mix of Asian and Western dishes. $

Above: tantalising oven-baked cod by Au Jardin Les Amis

NIGHTLIFE

The entertainment scene in Singapore has undergone a remarkable transformation in recent years from its previously staid image. In keeping with its new image as a global city, Singapore's nightlife options, once described as bland and boring, are suddenly hip and happening. And the kudos are not just coming from within: *Time* magazine ran an eight-page article called 'Singapore Swings'; and the *New York Times*, in its arts and leisure section, praised the city's explosive arts scene. Whether your tastes run to a refined evening at the ballet or a night of nonstop pub crawling, the options are plentiful.

Theatre, Dance and Music

Singapore aspires to be a city of the arts; and the dance, music and theatre scenes are all active. Check the schedules of the **Singapore Symphony Orchestra** (tel: 6338 1230; www.sso.org.sg), the **Singapore Dance Theatre** (tel: 6338 0611; www.singaporedancetheatre.com), especially the Ballet Under the Stars series, known affectionately as BUMS, and with the following theatre companies: **Action Theatre** (tel: 6837 0842; www.action.org.sg), **Necessary Stage** (tel: 6440 8115; www.necessary.org), **Theatreworks** (tel: 6737 7213; www.

theatreworks.org.sg) and the **Singapore Repertory Theatre** (tel: 6221 5585; www.srt.com.sg).

Singapore's superb arts centre, **The Esplanade – Theatres on the Bay** (tel: 6828 8377.; www.esplanade.com.sg) hosts a jam-packed calendar of both local and foreign productions all year round. **The Substation** (tel: 6337 7535; www.substation.org) has more experimental works while the more intimate **The Arts House** (tel: 6332 6900; www.the artshouse.com.sg) plays to smaller audiences.

Visiting companies add to the many options, and the annual Comedy and International arts festivals in March/April and June/July respectively provide a veritable feast for the senses. The daily papers give comprehensive listings of what's on, and free publications like *IS Magazine* and *This Week in Singapore* are all good sources. A good website source is livelife.ecitizen.gov.sg.

Tickets are sold by SISTIC (tel: 6348 5555 or www.sistic.com.sg) or Ticketcharge (tel: 6296 2929 or www.ticketcharge.com.sg).

Bars/Pubs/Clubs

If you don't fancy having to choose from a street full of bars and clubs, head instead to the in-house bars at the big hotels. Swissôtel the Stamford has **City Space** (tel: 6431 5669), which attracts jazz and cigar aficionados, and the vertigo-inducing **New Asia Bar** (tel: 6431 5669) on its 71st floor, while Raffles Hotel's **Long Bar** (tel: 6412 1229) is *the* place to try the original Singapore Sling. Another good option is the stylish **Post Bar** (tel: 6877 8135) at the Fullerton Hotel. Its bar menu includes a dizzying array of martinis.

If you are game for more interesting finds or more pub-crawling choices, read on. Most nightlife hubs are just a quick taxi ride away.

Note: the distinction between a disco and a bar is a blurred one these days: the best nightspots are invariably bars with a dance floor at one corner, either with a live band or a DJ spinning music.

Orchard Road

Nightspots along Orchard Road, unlike other areas in the city, are more spread out.

Alley Bar
Peranakan Place Complex
180 Orchard Road
Tel: 6732 6966
A stylish, sophisticated bar nestled – where else – in a cavernous alley. A big favourite with yuppies, many of whom drape themselves over its 15-m (49-ft)-long black terrazzo bar to enjoy cocktails such as mojitos and margaritas.

Bar None
Basement, Singapore Marriott Hotel
320 Orchard Road
Tel: 6831 4657
A long-time fixture on the nightlife circuit. Jive Talkin', the resident band, has a strong following with the local party crowd. Wild theme parties on some nights.

Brix
Basement, Grand Hyatt Singapore
10–12 Scotts Road
Tel: 6416 7107
Sophisticated watering hole featuring a three-level wine, whisky and music bar. Excellent selection of beers and cocktails and live band entertainment. Special theme parties every night of the week.

Ice Cold Beer
9 Emerald Hill
Tel: 6735 9929

The name says it all – this is the place to savour ice-cold beer. The jumbo-sized hot dogs are perfect with beer.

Muddy Murphy's Irish Pub
B1-04 Orchard Hotel Shopping Arcade
442 Orchard Road
Tel: 6735 0400
A thriving Dublin-style pub where taps flow with Guinness and Kilkenny. There's standing room only on most Friday nights.

Que Pasa
7 Emerald Hill Road
Tel: 6235 6626
Located in a quaint Peranakan-style townhouse in Emerald Hill, this Spanish-inspired bar serves a good range of drinks, including sangria. Delicious *tapas* are served to keep the hunger pangs at bay.

Rouge
Peranakan Place Complex
180 Orchard Road
Tel: 6732 6966
An excellent place for live music by the resident band Krueger and its frontman John Molina from 10.30pm on weekdays and 11pm on Saturday. Closed on Sunday.

The Living Room
01-00, Singapore Marriott Hotel
320 Orchard Road
Tel: 6831 4506
Complete with paintings, chandeliers and faux fireplace, this 'Victorian modern' living room is the place to relax to chill-out and lounge music.

Right: Raffles Hotel's world-famous Singapore Sling

Mohamed Sultan/River Valley

The area is where the serious party animals congregate. Several establishments along Mohamed Sultan Road provide a range of styles and decibel levels in conserved shophouses while several others are at Robertson Walk or nearby UE Square. The turnover is rapid, with places closing and new ones opening within months. Among the more enduring are the following.

Dbl O

01-24 Robertson Walk, 11 Unity Street
Tel: 6735 2008
Located at the corner of Mohamed Sultan Road and Unity Street, this nightspot plays an eclectic mix of disco, house, garage and retro music and has ample dance space. Sliding walls and a high ceiling give it a nice airy feel.

Next Page

17 Mohamed Sultan Road
Tel: 6235 6967
All done up in stylish dark wood with a strong Oriental theme and music with a strong retro slant. Features extra long happy hours from 3–9pm nightly.

The Liquid Room

01-05 The Gallery Hotel, 76 Robertson Quay
Tel: 6333 8117
Separated into two levels, the first floor Soundbar @ Liquid Room (with an alfresco area) is where you can listen to down-tempo beats. Upstairs is where all the action is. The club plays mainly trance and progressive house and has hosted several famous Japanese and international DJs.

Zouk/Velvet Underground

Jiak Kim Street
Tel: 6738 2988
Located some distance away from the main River Valley party scene but definitely worth the trudge there. One of Singapore's more enduring clubs with regular appearances by guest celebrity DJs. Zouk's brand of trance and techno is always a hit with its young crowd, while the adjoining Velvet Underground caters to a more mature audience. So well known it has made the news in several international publications.

Chijmes

Once a thriving public school and Catholic chapel, this historic area has been tastefully restored and is now a thriving nightlife hub with restaurants and bars. The fountain courtyard is a nice place to linger.

Father Flanagan's

B1-06 Chijmes, 30 Victoria Street
Tel: 6333 1418
An Irish pub that is hugely popular. Serves a good range of frothy ales and lagers and comforting dishes including smoked bacon soup, Irish stew, and beef and Guinness pie. Music from U2 and Van Morrison lend credence to the strong Irish atmosphere.

Insomnia Bar & Restaurant
01-21 Chijmes, 30 Victoria Street
Tel: 6338 6883
With good retro music by live bands in a stylish setup, this is the place to dance the night away. Features an international menu.

Boat Quay

Boat Quay and nearby Clarke Quay have a special ambience, situated just beside the Singapore River. Both areas attract a good crowd, especially at weekends, as much for their alfresco restaurants as for their bars housed in quaint old-style shophouses.

Bar Opiume
1 Empress Place
Tel: 6339 2876
Not quite Boat Quay but just across the river at the Asian Civilisations Museum. Draws a hip crowd with its jasmine-incensed modern minimalist interior and huge terrace; ideal for watching the river-boats go by.

BQ Bar
39 Boat Quay
Tel: 6536 9722
A mixed crowd of locals and expats come here for its laid-back house and jazz tunes and reasonably priced drinks. Complimentary bar snacks including olives, carrot and celery sticks and bruschetta with your drinks.

Harry's Bar
28 Boat Quay
Tel: 6538 3029
A good place for live jazz, and so popular that the action often spills out onto the road. Highly recommended. Achieved a certain notoriety as it was the favourite hang-out of Nick Leeson, the trader who brought the venerable Barings Bank to its knees.

Molly Malone's
56 Circular Road
Tel: 6536 2029
Like a scene straight out of Dublin, with Guinness and Kilkenny on tap, as well as decent pub grub and foot-stomping Irish music.

Clarke Quay

Over 30 restaurants and bars are found here. The nearest MRT station is Clarke Quay.

Attica
01-13/13/14 Clarke Quay
3A River Valley Road
Tel: 6333 9973
Attica's open courtyard setting with lush greenery and a fountain is the perfect setting to unwind to Latin, jazz and funk.

Brewerkz
01-05/ Riverside Point, 30 Merchant Road
Tel: 6438 7438
www.brewerkz.com
This is a micro-brewery, pub and restaurant modelled after versions in North America. There are six types of beer brewed, but the India Pale Ale is the local hit and best washes down the pub-type snacks.

Café Iguana
01-03 Riverside Point, 30 Merchant Road
Tel: 6236 1275
Right next door to Brewerkz is Café Iguana. Pop in if you feel like sampling over 100 different tequilas – just not all at once. Their margaritas are recommended and wine is available too, along with Tex-Mex cuisine.

Crazy Elephant
01-03/04 Clarke Quay
3E River Valley Road
Tel: 6337 1990
This small, smoky den is always full of people grooving to the great house band playing passionate jazz and heartfelt blues. The outdoor tables are usually busy, but they're the nicest places to sample the pizzas, pastas and sandwiches.

Ministry of Sound
01-12 Block C The Cannery, Clarke Quay
River Valley Road
Tel: 6235 2292
Dance to hip-hop, R&B, trance and house music. At 3,700 sq metre (40,000 sq ft), this is the biggest MOS worldwide.

1 Nite Stand Bar & Comedy Club
01-15 Clarke Quay
Tel: 6334 1954
A place to down a beer while laughing your head off at some of the best international comedians who fly in to entertain every last Wednesday to Saturday nights of the month.

Left: Chijmes – a thriving nightlife hub

CALENDAR OF EVENTS

Given the mix of races and religions, it is not surprising that Singapore's annual calendar is packed with festivals. Although the dates of ethnic festivals vary because they are based on the lunar calendar, most are confined to one or two specific months of the year.

The only exception is the Muslim festival of **Hari Raya Puasa**, which advances by a month or so each year. The festival celebrates the end of Ramadan, the fasting month in which no food or drink is consumed from dawn to dusk. During Ramadan, visit Bussorah Street where food stalls are set up each evening to cater to Muslims breaking their fast. Over at Geylang, in the east, a festive market-like atmosphere pervades in the evenings when coloured lights are switched on and vendors sell food and other products.

The other Muslim festival celebrated with a public holiday here is **Hari Raya Haji**, which marks the sacrifices made by Muslims who undertake the pilgrimage to Mecca and the mandatory giving of alms.

January/February

Weeks before the **Lunar New Year**, the most important festival for the Chinese, Chinatown is decked out in coloured lights and red and gold decorations. A colourful parade with dances and floats called Chingay is held on the 15th day.

Also during this period is the Indian harvest festival of **Ponggal**. In Indian homes, a pot of rice is allowed to boil over to symbolise prosperity, and food is offered to the gods in the Sri Perumal Temple in Serangoon Road.

Then comes the Indian festival of **Thaipusam**. Devotees carry enormous arched structures called *kavadi* along a 3km (1¾-mile) route from the Sri Perumal Temple in Serangoon Road to the Chettiar Temple in Tank Road. The *kavadi* are decorated with peacock feathers and held in place by hooks and skewers which pierce the bodies of the faithful who have prepared themselves with prayer and fasting.

March/April

Good Friday, which precedes Easter, is observed at many Christian churches in Singapore. In Catholic churches, the crucifixion of Jesus Christ is enacted and candle-lit processions are often held.

Also around this time the Chinese observe **Qing Ming** in remembrance of deceased ancestors and loved ones. Graves are tidied for the occasion and incense sticks, 'hell' money and paper gifts are burnt as offerings.

The **World Gourmet Summit**, which embodies the local love of food, comes with exhibitions and special menus.

The **Singapore International Comedy Festival** has stand-up and cabaret acts in various places around town, while the **Film Festival**'s non-mainstream offerings are a refreshing change for a population fed by a constant diet of Hollywood-made movies.

May/June/July

Vesak Day commemorates Buddha's birth, enlightenment and death. Prayers and meditation take place at the temples, followed by the release of caged birds.

Ritual celebrations for the **Birthday of the Third Prince**, a child god, are held in Chinese temples in May, with gory scenes of mediums in trance cutting themselves with swords and smearing their blood on paper for devotees.

The **Dragon Boat Festival** in June sees exciting races between teams from all over the world paddling across Marina Bay. It

Above: stacks of paper money to be offered to the Chinese gods
Right: colourful lanterns on display during Mooncake Festival

is held in remembrance of the poet Qu Yuan, who drowned himself in protest against political corruption in China.

The annual **Singapore Arts Festival** brings top-rate performers from around the world. Fringe and street events spill over to parks and shopping centres.

The Great Singapore Sale from end May to mid July each year is an island-wide shopping extravaganza. Many stores offer big mark-downs and special discounts during this period.

Another gastronomic event in July is the **Singapore Food Festival**, which feeds the locals' passion for food.

August/September

August is an important month. To celebrate **National Day** on 9 August, a parade and mass displays are held either at the Padang or National Stadium and the evening ends with a fireworks display.

The Chinese believe the gates of hell open during the seventh lunar month, the **Chinese Hungry Ghosts** month, allowing ghosts to visit the physical world. To placate the wandering ghosts, incense sticks and hell money are burned and food is offered. Temporary stage shows or *getai* spring up around town with stage performances and auctions of auspicious items.

The **Mooncake Festival** takes place soon after the seventh month and coincides with what is believed to be the year's brightest full moon during the eighth lunar month. Children carry lanterns and adults drink tea and partake of mooncakes filled with lotus seed paste.

October

Little India (Serangoon Road) and Indian homes glow with lighted oil lamps and garlands in celebration of the most important Hindu festival here – **Deepavali**, when the powers of light triumph over darkness. During this month also is the **Festival of Navarathiri**, when Indian temples become venues for classical dance and musical performances in honour of Dhurga, Lakshmi and Saraswathi, the consorts of the Hindu Trinity.

The **Thimithi Festival**, also in October, is something to watch out for. Fire-walking in honour of the goddess Draupadi, heroine of the *Mahabharata* epic who walked on fire to prove her chastity, takes place at the Sri Mariamman Temple at South Bridge Road.

Kusu Island is the destination for Chinese and Muslim pilgrims from mid-October to mid-November. According to legend, two fishermen were carried to safety on the island on the back of a giant turtle, which rescued them after their boat sank.

The Chinese festival of the **Nine Emperor Gods**, during which the divine powers are said to cure all ills and bestow good fortune on their nine-day visit to Earth, is celebrated with *wayang* (Chinese opera) and a procession with the effigies of the gods borne aloft on sedan chairs.

November/December

Orchard Road lights up for **Christmas** on 25 December, and the year winds up with carols being sung in the streets and parties.

Practical Information

GETTING THERE

By Air

The **Singapore Changi Airport** (tel: 6541 2267; www.changiairport.com.sg), consistently polled the world's best airport by travellers and businessmen, is spacious and awash in greenery. There are work spaces for laptops, business centres, an airport hotel, a gym and prayer rooms; and improvements and new facilities are constantly being added. Baggage handling is quick and there are always taxis waiting to whisk arriving passengers to the city.

Changi has at present three terminals – Terminal 1 (T1), Terminal 2 (T2) and the Budget Terminal (tel: 6412 7500; www.btsingapore.com). When completed in 2008, Terminal 3 will expand the airport's handling capacity from 25 to 60 million passengers a year.

The terminals offer a tremendous assortment of duty-free shops, food outlets, pubs and entertainment options. T1 is the older of the two terminals, but has almost identical 'activities' as T2. The Budget Terminal's (BT) offerings are basic, but its passengers can easily connect to T2 and its amenities using the BT Shuttle Service, available 24 hours daily. Passengers can also shuttle between T1 and T2 by the Sky Train service (daily 6–1.30am).

Changi Airport is linked directly to 184 cities in 57 countries, with 80 airlines operating over 4,000 flights a week. The award-winning **Singapore Airlines** (www.singaporeair.com) flies to over 62 cities worldwide and its sister airline **SilkAir** (www.silkair.com) serves 26 destinations in Asia.

By Sea

Most visitors who come by boat arrive at the **Singapore Cruise Centre** (tel: 6513 2200; www.singaporecruise.com) located at the **HarbourFront Centre**. Singapore-based cruise liners sail to various countries in the region and also offer one-way cruise options. Contact **Star Cruises** (tel: 6226 1168; www.starcruises.com) for more information.

Tanah Merah Ferry Terminal (tel: 6545 2048), located near Changi Airport, has ferry services to Bintan and Batam islands in Indonesia and also to Tioman island in Malaysia.

Nearby, **Changi Ferry Terminal** (tel: 6214 8031) handles regular ferry services to Tanjung Belungkor, Johor, from which land transfer to Desaru can be arranged.

By Road

Singapore is accessible by road from Ipoh and Kuala Lumpur on the west coast, and Kota Bharu on the east. It takes about 5 hours to drive from Kuala Lumpur (KL) via the North-South Highway. Travelling via Johor Bahru, entry into Singapore is either through the Woodlands Checkpoint in the north of Singapore or the Tuas Second Link in the west. Several private bus companies and travel agents in Singapore operate air-conditioned bus services to Malaysia and southern Thailand. **Gunung Raya Travel**, at 01-13 Golden Mile Complex, 5001 Beach Road, has frequent daily departures (tel: 6294 7711; www.gunungraya.com).

By Rail

A railway line links Singapore to Kuala Lumpur (KL), Butterworth and Bangkok, as well as to Tumpat, near Kota Bharu. Enquire at the **KTM Station** at Keppel Road (tel: 6222 5165; www.ktmb.com.my).

The **Eastern & Orient Express** plies the 1,900-km (1,200-mile) route linking Bangkok, KL and Singapore. The journey takes three days and fares start at US$1,490 per person (tel: 6392 3500; www.orient-express.com).

Left: Marriott Hotel and Tangs department store
Right: world-famous Eastern Oriental Express

TRAVEL ESSENTIALS

Climate

As Singapore is situated just 137km (85 miles) north of the Equator, the weather usually varies between hot and very hot. Maximum daytime temperatures seldom exceed 33°C (91°F) and rarely drop below 23°C (73°F) at night. Most of the rain falls during the northeast monsoon between November and February and to a lesser degree during the southwest monsoon from May to September. Thunderstorms, though, can occur throughout the year. Humidity levels range between 64 and 98 percent.

Visas

Visa requirements vary from time to time, so check with a Singapore embassy or consular office in your home country. Most visitors are automatically given a 30-day social visit pass on arrival. Application for renewals can be made at the **Immigration & Checkpoints Authority** (ICA) 10 Kallang Road. For details, call the hotline: 6391 6100; www.ica.gov.sg.

Money Matters

The local currency consists of notes in $2, $5, $10, $50, $100, $500, $1,000 and $10,000 denominations. Coins are in denominations of 1, 5, 10, 20, 50 cents and $1. One Singapore Dollar is roughly equivalent to about US$1.58 at time of press. There are no restrictions on the amount of currency you can bring into the country. Generally, licensed money-changers found in shopping malls offer the best rates. International charge and credit cards are widely accepted.

What to Wear

Smart-casual gear will see you through most occasions in Singapore, where normal office attire is shirt and tie, with jackets being reserved for more formal occasions. Dress to cope with the heat when outdoors and have a wrap or light cardigan for the sharp drop in temperature inside some air-conditioned buildings. Shorts and t-shirts are acceptable in many places, although many clubs and discos and some restaurants have stricter dress codes.

Electricity

Electrical supply is on a 220–240 volt, 50 Hz system. Most hotels have transformers for 110–120 volt, 60 Hz appliances.

Airport Tax

Passengers departing from Changi Airport's T1 and T2 have to pay a S$21 tax. A S$13 tax is levied for those leaving from the Budget Terminal. This tax is usually incorporated into your airline ticket; if not, it has to be paid during check-in.

GETTING ACQUAINTED

Geography

The Republic of Singapore consists of the main island, about 699sq km (267sq miles) in area, and 58 other smaller islands, located at the southern tip of peninsular Malaysia. The shape of the island has changed over the years through land reclamation. The highest point is Bukit Timah Hill at 162m (530ft) with most of the main island less than 15m (50ft) above sea level.

Government and Economy

A unicameral government with general elections held once every five years. The People's Action Party (PAP) has been in power since independence in 1965. Lee Hsien Loong has been Prime Minister since 2004. The mainstays of the economy are manufacturing, finance and business services, commerce, transport and communications, tourism and construction.

Singapore's per capita GNP of S$37,656 (in 2002) makes it the second richest country in Asia after Japan.

Population and Religion

Singapore's population is over 4.3 million, with 76 percent Chinese, 14 percent Malay, 8 percent Indian and 2 percent 'others' (such as Eurasians and Caucasians). The majority of Chinese practise Buddhism and/or Taoism and there is a growing minority of Christians. Malays are generally Muslim and Indians are either Hindu, Sikh or Christian.

Time

Singapore is 8 hours ahead of GMT.

practical information

Tipping
Most hotel and restaurant bills come with a 10 percent service charge on top of a 5 percent Goods and Services (GST) tax and a 1 percent 'cess' charge, which goes to fund tourism. Tipping is not expected, but is appreciated in cases of special effort.

Tourist Information
There's a wealth of free literature at the airport, hotels, shopping centres and tourist attractions. Your hotel concierge is also a good source of information.

The **Singapore Tourism Board** (24-hour infoline: 1800-736 2000; www.visitsingapore.com) has visitor centres at the following locations: **Orchard Road**; **Liang Court**; **InnCrowd Backpackers' Hostel** in Little India; **Suntec City Mall**; **Singapore Cruise Centre** and **Changi Airport Terminals 1 and 2**.

Goods and Services Tax
A **GST** of 5 percent is charged on most purchases, which is refundable for visitors who make purchases from shops participating in the **Global Refund Scheme** and the **Premier Tax Free Scheme**, which display 'Tax Free Shopping' and 'Premier Tax Free' stickers respectively. The refund applies to purchases exceeding S$100. Show your passport to the retailer and fill out a voucher. Before departure, validate the voucher at the airport customs, then present it together with your purchased items at the **Global Refund Counter** (tel: 6225 6238) or **Premier Tax Free Scheme Counter** (tel:

1800-829 3733). You can opt for cash or a refund back to your credit card.

Etiquette
Most good behaviour in Singapore is law-enforced; public signage in the country is usually very good and there are clear signs explaining what to do and what not to do. Littering can cost you up to S$1,000; smoking in most non-smoking public places, including government offices, air-conditioned restaurants, cinemas and supermarkets, S$1,000; and using the mobile phone while driving is liable to a fine of up to S$1,000. You can now buy chewing gum in Singapore – albeit only gum with 'therapeutic' value, such as that deemed beneficial to oral health.

There is no fine, thankfully, for forgetting to remove your shoes before entering a mosque, Indian temple or an Asian home. When keeping company with Muslims and Hindus, neither eat with nor offer anything with your left hand.

Singapore is very cosmopolitan, and, even if you are unfamiliar with the finer points of etiquette here, courteous behaviour and a smile should ensure your smooth passage throughout. For deeper insights, look out for JoAnn Meriwether Craig's *Culture Shock in Singapore*.

GETTING AROUND

From the airport
There are several ways to make your way to town from the airport. Some hotels also provide a shuttle service for their guests.

The **taxi** stands at Changi Airport are well organised. The 20-minute trip (barring peak-hour traffic) to the city on the East Coast Parkway (ECP) should cost about S$25, including surcharges.

The Airport Shuttle Service's **Maxicabs** carry a maximum of six passengers at a time; pick-up is just outside the arrival hall. The fares are S$7 (adult) and S$5 (child) and you can ask to be dropped off at any hotel in the city.

The MRT link from the airport to the City Hall Station downtown takes about 30 minutes and costs S$1.50.

Above: signs of Singapore

A slew of surcharges apply: advance bookings; ERP (Electronic Road Pricing), midnight (between 11.30pm–6am), extra baggage, peak-hour (am and pm); airport surcharge of S$3 or S$5 (5pm–midnight Fri–Sun) for taxis that depart the airport. Confused? Even Singaporeans cannot keep up with the list of extra charges. Most tend to trust the taxi drivers; they are generally honest. Even with the extras, taxis in Singapore are inexpensive.

Car Rental and ERP

Avis (tel: 6737 1668) and **Hertz** (tel: 1800-734 4646) offer both self-drive and chauffeur-driven cars. You will need a valid driving licence. Driving is on the left and seat belts are compulsory. More importantly, have an understanding of the **Electronic Road Pricing** (ERP) system before you drive. During peak hours, the ERP scheme controls traffic flow into the Central Business District (CBD) and on major expressways. There is a scale of charges applicable to different periods and vehicle types. Current charges are indicated on electronic boards just before an ERP gantry. When you drive through an ERP gantry, it will automatically deduct the correct fee from the cash card inserted into a special gadget in your car. Pre-paid

The airport is also served by air-conditioned **buses**, the stands for which are located in the basement: an option for those with time and minimal luggage.

Taxis

The easiest way to see Singapore is by taxi. There are more than 18,000 taxis plying the roads and most drivers speak or understand basic English. Generally, cabs can be hailed off the streets or at taxi stands. During peak hours, or when it's raining, booking a taxi is the best option: call **Comfort** (tel: 6552 1111), **CityCab** (tel: 6552 2222) or **SMRT** (tel: 6555 8888). Flag-down fare starts from S$2.50 for the first kilometre, and most taxis accept credit cards.

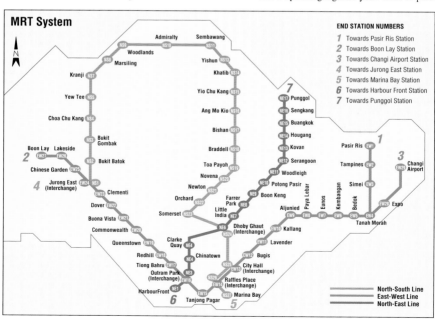

MRT System

N

END STATION NUMBERS

1 Towards Pasir Ris Station
2 Towards Boon Lay Station
3 Towards Changi Airport Station
4 Towards Jurong East Station
5 Towards Marina Bay Station
6 Towards Harbour Front Station
7 Towards Punggol Station

North-South Line
East-West Line
North-East Line

cash cards are available at post offices or petrol stations; most car rental companies will also sell you one.

Buses

Efficient bus services operated by **SBS Transit** and **SMRT** cover most of the island and operate from 6am–midnight. Fares are S$0.80 to S$1.50 for non-air-conditioned buses and S$0.90 to S$1.80 for air-conditioned buses.

Be sure to have the exact fare as bus drivers do not give change. For convenience, buy a S$15 EZ-link card with a refundable S$3 deposit. This allows cashless payment on all public buses and the MRT *(see below)*. By using the EZ-link card, commuters can also enjoy lower fares and rebates when transferring between trains and buses.

Tap your card on the electronic reader located at the bus entrance (or turnstile at the MRT station), which then automatically deducts the maximum fare. When alighting from the bus or disembarking from the train, tap the card again on the reader at the exit, and the unused fare portion will be credited back into the card.

EZ-link cards are sold at Transitlink offices at all MRT stations and bus interchanges. When the value of your card runs low, you can top it up at these same offices.

A useful purchase is the Translink Guide. Priced at S$2, this pocket-sized book includes detailed information on all bus routes and MRT services. For information on bus and MRT routes, and all related enquiries call the Translink Hotline 1800-225 5663.

MRT

Singapore's Mass Rapid Transit (MRT) is the envy of commuters everywhere. With the opening of the North-East Line, 16 stations have been added to the existing 50-station network on the East-West and North-South lines. Trains operate from 5.30am till 12.30am and fares range from S$0.90 to S$1.90. Trains run at intervals of 2–8 minutes depending on the time of travel.

The price of a single-trip ticket dispensed by ticket machines include a S$1 deposit. This is refunded by the ticket machine at the end of your trip. This can be a bother, so if you plan to uses buses and the MRT for several trips, buy instead a stored-value EZ-link

card *(see above)*. Using the train is easy, just tap your card on the electronic readers at the start and end of your trip as you do on buses.

Work on the new Circle Line is in progress and it's scheduled for completion in 2010.

Strict laws prohibiting eating and littering ensure spotless stations and carriages so keep your litter with you until you alight.

Singapore Trolley

Singapore Explorer (tel: 6339 6833; www.singaporeexplorer.com.sg) operates novel wood-trimmed buses that ply between the main hotels and tourist attractions, with 17 stops along the way. Unlimited travel all day costs S$9 (adult) and S$7 (child). Buy your ticket from your hotel concierge or direct from the driver.

Trishaws

Although mainly used by tourist groups, you can hire a trishaw on your own. Just make sure you agree on the destination and fare before starting out. A tour of the city, lasting 20–30 minutes, will cost S$25–30. Turn up at the trishaw station behind Bugis Village next to Fu Lu Shou Complex where trishaws congregate between 5 and 11pm, It is safer to use trishaws only after 8pm, when the flow of heavy traffic has eased. Enquire at your hotel reception desk, or call **Singapore Explorer** (tel: 6339 6833) for more information.

SIA Hop-on

The **SIA Hop-on** is a tourist bus service that operates unlimited rides to the various attractions in the city. It stops along major hotels, shopping malls and landmarks. Tickets cost S$12 (adult) and S$6 (child). Singapore Airlines and SilkAir passengers visiting Singapore pay S$3. Tickets are available from most hotels or directly

Left Top: interior of MRT trains
Right: Singapore Trolley

practical information

from the bus driver. Contact **SH Tours** (tel: 6734 9923; www.asiatours.com.sg) for information.

Boats

A cruise on a local 'bumboat' is a novel way of taking in the sights along the Singapore River. Operated by **Singapore River Cruises** (tel: 6336 6111 or 6336 6119; www.rivercruise.com.sg), the boats ply two routes: tickets for the 30-minute route costs S\$12 while the longer 45-minute route costs S\$15. Tickets can be purchased at the jetties alongside Merlion Park, Esplanade, Boat Quay, Liang Court (near Clarke Quay) and the Raffles Landing Site. You can return to where you boarded or get off at any of the stops along the way (just let the boat driver know beforehand).

Tours

RMG Tours (tel: 6220 8722); **Singapore Sightseeing** (tel: 6336 9011); **SH Tours** (tel: 6734 9923); **Holiday Tours** (tel: 6738 2622) operate half- and full-day tours. Apart from the usual tours, these companies also operate themed tours which focus on cuisine, *feng shui* (Chinese geomancy), colonial history and other aspects of Singapore (check www.visitsingapore.com for details).

Journeys' Original Singapore Walks (tel: 6325 1631; www.singaporewalks.com) take you on eclectic walking tours, including visits to Chinatown, Little India, 'wet' markets, graveyards, funeral shops, and even (supposedly) haunted houses.

Journeys also offers a coach tour that includes visits to the Changi Museum, Changi Beach and Changi Village *(see Itinerary 8 on page 48).*

ACCOMMODATION

Hotels in Singapore rate among the best in the world in terms of service, comfort and amenities. Note that prices are subject to 10 percent service charge and 5 percent GST.

If you arrive at Changi airport without booking a room, head for the **Singapore Hotel Association** counters (daily 7.30am–11.30pm) at Changi Airport's Terminal 1 or 2, or the Budget Terminal. Rack rates for double rooms have been grouped under the following price categories:

$$$$ = S\$300 and above,
$$$ = S\$200–299,
$$ = S\$100–199,
$ = S\$99 and below.

$$$$

Conrad Centennial Singapore
2 Temasek Boulevard
Tel: 6338 8830; Fax: 6432 7198
www.conradhotels.com
Five-star hotel closest to Suntec City. Big luxurious rooms with windows overlooking picturesque Marina Bay. Excellent choice for businessmen with its wide range of facilities and fine restaurants.

Four Seasons
190 Orchard Boulevard
Tel: 6734 1110; Fax: 6733 0682
www.fourseasons.com/singapore
Intimate property (254 rooms) with a marbled foyer and scattered with exquisite artworks. Impeccable service amid an atmosphere of understated luxury.

Fullerton Hotel
1 Fullerton Square
Tel: 6733 8388; Fax: 6735 8388
www.fullertonhotel.com
This historical jewel of a building was restored and transformed into a luxury hotel in 2000. The colonnaded exterior gives way to a surprisingly contemporary interior filled with art deco furniture. A

Left: Raffles Hotel

variety of room styles plus the highly regarded San Marco at the Lighthouse and Jade restaurants.

Goodwood Park
22 Scotts Road
Tel: 6737 7411; Fax: 6732 8558
www.goodwoodparkhotel.com.sg
A national landmark with loads of colonial-era charm, set back from the bustle of Scotts Road amid tropical greenery. Excellent restaurants and within walking distance from Orchard Road.

Grand Hyatt
10–12 Scotts Road
Tel: 6738 1234; Fax: 6732 1696
www.singapore.hyatt.com
A stone's throw from Orchard Road, the sophisticated Grand Hyatt impresses with its minimalist, almost stark décor and excellent service. Has a 24-hour coffee house and restaurants serving Chinese, Italian and international cuisines. Beautiful pool area is reminiscent of a beach resort.

Intercontinental Singapore
80 Middle Road
Tel: 6338 7600; Fax: 6338 7366
www.intercontinental.com
Stylish hotel with a distinct tropical charm. Driveway discreetly tucked away from the main road. Well-appointed rooms in the tower block and smaller retro-style rooms in the old shophouse block. Conveniently located near an MRT station and the adjoining Bugis Junction shopping mall.

Mandarin Singapore
333 Orchard Road
Tel: 6737 4411; Fax: 6732 2361
www.mandarin-singapore.com
With a good reputation for service and a prime location on Orchard Road, the Mandarin is favoured by business travellers and serious shoppers. Its Top of the M, Singapore's highest revolving restaurant, has sweeping city views.

Raffles
1 Beach Road
Tel: 6337 1886; Fax: 6339 7650
www.raffleshotel.com

The Grand Dame of historical Asian hotels. Guests stay in suites and are cocooned in a private, genteel world where one is greeted by name and treads on wooden floors lined with antique rugs while gazing at museum-quality art pieces. The private pool is open 24 hours and bathrooms are designed for absolute indulgence.

Ritz-Carlton Millenia
7 Raffles Avenue
Tel: 6337 8888; Fax: 6338 0001
www.ritzcarlton.com/hotels/singapore
The sheer luxury hits you the moment you step into the foyer, with its contemporary design and marble-clad spaces studded with Dale Chihuly glass sculptures. In the rooms, the décor is understated luxury, but the *pièce de résistance* must surely be the oversized bathrooms with huge picture windows by the bathtubs.

Shangri-La
22 Orange Grove Road
Tel: 6737 3644; Fax: 6733 1029
www.shangri-la.com
This garden paradise deserves its billing as Singapore's other botanic garden, with flowers spilling over balconies and along the corridors. The grand foyer is always busy in spite of its location away from the main thoroughfares. Excellent service and luxuriously furnished rooms, with fine restaurants, including Blu, a chic bar and restaurant serving Californian cuisine.

Swissôtel The Stamford
2 Stamford Road
Tel: 6338 8585; Fax: 6338 2862
www.singapore-stamford.swissotel.com
The city's major attractions are either within walking distance or can be reached by MRT in minutes from the 70-storey Swissôtel. It commands stunning views from its higher floors while the adjacent Raffles the Plaza (80 Bras Basah Road; tel: 6337 1554) is an excellent business hotel.

$$$
Berjaya Hotel (formerly Duxton)
83 Duxton Road
Tel: 6227 7678; Fax: 6227 1232
www.berjayaresorts.com

A boutique hotel (48 rooms) with a five-star feel and a off-centre location in Tanjong Pagar, a post-war conservation area. Intimate and exclusive, and close to the business district. There are good pubs and excellent restaurants in the vicinity.

Hotel Rendezvous
9 Bras Basah Road
Tel: 6336 0220; Fax: 6337 3773
www.rendezvoushotels.com
This four-star domed hotel is located close to the Singapore Art Museum, halfway between the Civic District and Orchard Road. Has a pool, fitness and spa centre. Rendezvous Restaurant will delight diners with its famous spicy *nasi padang* (Indonesian-style rice and curries).

Phoenix
277 Orchard Road
Tel: 6737 8666; Fax: 6732 2024
www.hotelphoenixsingapore.com
Right on Singapore's entertainment and shopping belt, the Phoenix commands a great Orchard Road location for its price range. Extensively renovated city hotel with innovative room features, from personal computers, exercise equipment and massage couches to mini-TVs in the bathrooms.

$$
Hotel 1929
50 Keong Saik Road
Tel: 6347 1929; Fax: 6327 1929
www.hotel1929.com
Snuggled in the heart of Chinatown, this is a boutique property combining a mix of old-world Singapore architecture and nouveau chic style. No two rooms are designed the same way and many are embellished with unique furniture from the owner's private collection. Its Ember restaurant on the ground floor has won rave reviews for its suitably chic ambience and creative fusion cuisine.

Plaza Parkroyal
7500A Beach Road
Tel: 6298 0011; Fax: 6296 3600
www.parkroyalhotels.com
Sited near the traditional Malay and Indian commercial districts. Has an excellent health-fitness club with jacuzzi, and pool.

Robertson Quay
15 Merbau Road
Tel: 6735 3333; Fax: 6738 1515
www.robertsonquayhotel.com.sg
Simple little hotel on the Singapore River within a stone's throw of Mohamed Sultan Road, a nightlife hotspot. Rooms are small with compact bathrooms, but many have a lovely river view. A path just along the river leads to the dining and entertainment options in Clarke Quay and Boat Quay.

Royal Peacock
55 Keong Saik Road
Tel: 6223 3522; Fax: 6221 1770
www.royalpeacockhotel.com
Boutique hotel inspired by a Baroque theme and jewel-toned colours. Rooms have plush purple carpeting, red walls and wooden sleigh beds. Café and bar on site. Only a 10-minute walk to Outram Park MRT Station.

The Scarlet
33 Erskine Road
Tel: 6511 3333; Fax: 6511 3303
www.thescarlethotel.com
A boutique hotel that combines the charms of the Tanjong Pagar district with modern comforts. With characterful ensuite rooms, a gym and an open-air jacuzzi. A 10-minute walk to Tanjong Pagar MRT Station.

$
Hangout@Mt.Emily
10A Upper Wilkie Road
Tel: 6438 5588; Fax: 6339 6008
www.hangouthotels.com
New and funky budget-class hotel conveniently located near the Civic District. Clean and comfortable, though without frills. Located a 10-minute walk away from Dhoby Ghaut MRT Station.

Perak Hotel
12 Perak Road
Tel: 6299 7733; Fax: 6392 0919
www.peraklodge.net
Perak Hotel occupies a restored shophouse in a charming location in Little India. Lovely restaurant with friendly staff. Five minutes' walk from Bugis and Little India MRT stations. Rooms are ensuite with air-conditioning and TV; breakfast included.

HEALTH AND EMERGENCIES

Health

The local water off the tap is treated and safe for drinking. Singapore's clean, green image is a fact, largely because of zealous reinforcement by vigilant authorities. Strict control is exercised over the hygiene of food sold, from hawker stalls to hotels. However, if you've had one too many chilli crab, and require treatment, there are about 16 government and private hospitals as well as umpteen number of clinics for any eventuality. Singapore is fast gaining a reputation as a regional medical hub par excellence; the number of foreigners seeking treatment here, especially from Indonesia, is high. Consultation fees start from about S$30 in a private practice. The following hospitals are recommended.

Mount Elizabeth Hospital
3 Mount Elizabeth
Tel: 6737 2666; www.mountelizabeth.com.sg

Singapore General Hospital
Outram Road
Tel: 6222 3322; www.sgh.com.sg

BUSINESS HOURS

Business hours are 9am–5pm and banks are usually open 10am–3pm on weekdays, and 9.30–11am on Saturdays. Some also open on Sundays from 11am until 3pm. Shops open from about 10am to 8pm and many department stores are open until 9pm. Most shops are open on Sundays. Most Singapore Post branches in town are open from 8.30am to 6.30pm on weekdays and from 8.30am to 1pm on Saturdays.

PUBLIC HOLIDAYS

New Year's Day	1 January
Labour Day	1 May
Good Friday	April
Vesak Day	May
National Day	9 August
Christmas Day	25 December

Variable dates
  Hari Raya Puasa
  Chinese New Year (January/February)
  Hari Raya Haji
  Deepavali (October/November)

COMMUNICATIONS

Telephone and Postal Services

The country code for Singapore is 65 (there are no area codes). To call overseas from Singapore, dial the international access code 001 or for budget calls, either 013 or 019, followed by the relevant country code.

Mobile phone users with global roaming service should take note that the local network is GSM, common to most countries except Japan and the US. It may be more economical to buy a local SIM card from one of the three service providers: **Singtel** (tel: 1626 or 6738 0123), **M1** (tel: 1627 or 1800-843 8383) or **Starhub** (tel: 1633 or 6825 5000). These cards, which give you a local mobile number, cost a minimum of S$20 and can be topped up when the value falls. All local mobile numbers begin with an '8' or '9'.

Public telephones are easy to find and local calls cost 10 cents for every 3 minutes. Clearly marked phones can be used for worldwide calls. For convenience, buy S$3, S$5, S$10, S$20 or S$50 phone cards for both local and overseas calls. Increasingly, public phones which use coins are becoming a rare sight in Singapore.

Postal services are fast and efficient. An aerogramme to anywhere in the world costs 50 cents. Most hotels will handle mail for you or you may post letters and parcels yourself at any post office, where you may also send faxes. The **Singapore Post** branch at 1 Killiney Road is open Mon–Fri 8.30am–9pm, Sat 8.30am–4pm, and Sun and public holidays 9am–4.30pm; the branch at Changi Airport Terminal 2 is open 8am–9.30pm daily. Call 1605 for information about postal rates, express mail and other services.

Right: post-on-wheels

Internet Access

Among the many grand plans Singapore has laid out for itself is that of an intelligent island plugged into the global village. As such, Singaporeans are generallly a tech-savvy lot. Internet cafés can charge as low as S$1 per hour. Check with your hotel concierge to see if there is one close to your hotel.

Newspapers

The Straits Times and *The Business Times* are local English language dailies, carrying local and international news, with the tabloid *The New Paper* appearing in the afternoons. *Today*, a tabloid with morning and afternoon editions, is available free at MRT stations.

Foreign newspapers including the *International Herald Tribune, Financial Times* and *Asian Wall Street Journal* are available on the day of publication at the major business hotels and large bookshops.

Radio

English channels are One FM (90.5 MHz), Symphony 92 FM (92.4 MHz), News Radio 938 (93.8 MHz), Perfect 10 (98.7 MHz); Class 95 FM (95 MHz); Radio 91.3 (91.3 MHz); and Power 98 (98.0 MHz). The BBC World Service is on 88.9 MHz.

Television

MediaCorp provides the daily diet of local programming. In total, there are five channels: Channel 5, Central and Channel NewsAsia broadcast in English. Channel 5 offers mainly Western (ie American) fare, in addition to its own local productions. Central airs nature and travel documentaries, cultural programmes and art movies, as well as Tamil programmes. Channel NewsAsia offers useful news updates on the hour and current affairs shows in between. Channel 8 and Channel U broadcast in Mandarin and Suria in Malay. Some sets can also receive Malaysian RTM 1 and 2, and TV3.

Pay TV is available through Singapore Cable Vision (SCV), which offers over 40 TV channels 24 hours a day. Singapore is a hub for several foreign broadcasters which beam their programmes out of Singapore via satellite to regional and worldwide audiences.

SPORTS

Golf

Green fees range from S$40 for a nine-hole course on weekdays to S$400 for a full round at a championship course on weekends. Most golf and country clubs are open to visitors on weekdays. Some clubs may ask you for a proficiency certificate.

Changi Golf Club, 20 Netheravon Road, tel: 6545 5133. A nine-hole course. A big plus is its proximity to the sea.

Keppel Club, Bukit Chermin Road, tel: 6273 5522. An 18-hole course.

Raffles Country Club, 450 Jalan Ahmad Ibrahim, tel: 6861 7649. An 18-hole course.

Sentosa Golf Club, 27 Bukit Manis Road, Sentosa Island, tel: 6275 0090. An 18-hole course.

Tanah Merah Country Club, Changi Coast Road, tel: 6542 3040. Two 18-hole courses.

Warren Golf Club, 81 Chua Chu Kang Way, tel: 6586 1244. An 18-hole course.

Windsurfing

SAFYC Sea Sports Centre, 11 Changi Coast Walk, tel: 6546 5880, www.safyc.org.sg. Located near Tanah Merah Ferry Terminal, this centre offers windsurfing, kayaking and laser sailing. If you can get together with five other participants, you can join a weekend basic windsurfing course. There's a day fee of S$10 for use of the club. Rental fees for boats, kayaks and windsurf boards apply.

Waterskiing and Wakeboarding

Extreme Sports, Kallang Riverside Park, tel: 6334 8813, www.extreme.com.sg. You can both ski or wakeboard at Kallang River; it costs S$90 an hour on weekdays and S$120 on weekends, including equipment rental. Beginner lessons (4 sessions) cost S$150.

Punggol Sea Sports Accessories, 17th Avenue, 600 Punggol Road, tel: 6386 3891, www.pssa.com.sg. Offers water-skiing and wakeboarding; a boat with driver costs S$80–90 per hour.

Cycling

Bicycles may be hired by the hour at **East Coast Park**'s bike-hire kiosks and on

Sentosa Island where there is a 5-km (3-mile) track around the island. There are also several bike rental kiosks near the jetty on Pulau Ubin.

Tennis
Booking a tennis court costs about S$10.50 per hour, or more if you play in the evening under the lights. You may reserve tennis courts at the Singapore Tennis Centre (tel: 6442 5966; 1020 East Coast Parkway).

Horse Racing
Live racing as well as live telecasts of Malaysian races can be enjoyed at the Singapore Turf Club in Kranji in the north. A strict dress code is observed at the club. Singapore races are held on selected Friday nights and Saturday and Sunday afternoons. For details, call 6879 1000 or check www.turfclub.com.sg.

Bowling
There are several bowling alleys spread across the island, many of them in the suburbs and some open 24 hours. Shoes are available for hire and charges range between S$2 and S$4 per game. On weekends, reservations may be necessary.
Superbowl, Marina Grove, Marina South, tel: 6221 1010.

USEFUL NUMBERS

Fire and ambulance	995
Police	999
Flight information	1800-542 4422
Immigration & Checkpoints Authority	6391 6100
Meteorological Office	6542 7788
STB Touristline	1800-736 2000
Postal service	1605
CitySearch (operator-assisted Yellow Pages)	1900-777 7777
Directory assistance	100
Directory assistance (from public phone)	161
Overseas call booking	104
Time of day	1711
Operator assistance	100
Overseas call booking	104

USEFUL ADDRESSES

Airlines
Air France, 06-01/02/03, 79 Anson Road, tel: 6415 5111.
Air New Zealand, 24-08 Ocean Building, 10 Collyer Quay, tel: 6535 8266.
American Airlines, 10-03 Raffles City Tower, 250 North Bridge Road, tel: 800-189 1019.
BA/Qantas Airways, 06-05 Cairnhill Place, 15 Cairnhill Road, tel: 6589 7000.
Cathay Pacific Airways, 16-03 Ocean Building, 10 Collyer Quay, tel: 6533 1333.
Japan Airlines, Level 3, 16 Raffles Quay, Hong Leong Building, tel: 6221 0522.
KLM Royal Dutch Airlines, 06-01/02/03, 79 Anson Road, tel: 6823 2220.
Lufthansa Airlines, 05-01 Palais Renaissance, 390 Orchard Road, tel: 6245 5600.
Malaysia Airlines, 190 Clemenceau Avenue, 02-09/11 Singapore Shopping Centre, tel: 6336 6777.
Northwest Airlines, tel: 6336 3371 (no walk-ins).
Singapore Airlines, 02-38 The Paragon, 290 Orchard Road, tel: 6223 8888.
Thai International, 03-00, 100 Cecil Street, tel: 6210 5111.
United Airlines, 01-03 Hong Leong Building, 16 Raffles Quay, tel: 6873 3533.

Embassies
Australia, 25 Napier Road, tel: 6836 4100.
Britain, 100 Tanglin Road, tel: 6424 4200.
Canada, 11-01 One George Street, tel: 6854 5900.
France, 101–103 Cluny Park Road, tel: 6880 7800.
Germany, 12-00 Singapore Land Tower, 50 Raffles Place, tel: 6533 6002.
Italy, 27-02 United Square, 101 Thomson Road, tel: 6250 6022.
Japan, 16 Nassim Road, tel: 6235 8855.
New Zealand, 15-06 Ngee Ann City Tower A, 391A Orchard Road, tel: 6235 9966.
Switzerland, 1 Swiss Club Link, tel: 6468 5788.
USA, 27 Napier Road, tel: 6476 9100.

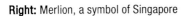

Right: Merlion, a symbol of Singapore

FURTHER READING

Clarence Plays the Numbers by Yen Chung. Landmark Books. Novel about a Eurasian civil servant in 1950s Singapore.

Fistful of Colours by Suchen Christine Lim. SNP. A multi-layered reflection of what it means to be Singaporean, through a single day in the life of Suwen, a young Chinese teacher.

Latent Images: Film in Singapore by Jan and Yvonne Uhde. Times. A well-documented study of film in Singapore, from the early days of local film production to cinema-going and film-making of the recent years.

Mammon Inc. by Tan Hwee Hwee. Penguin UK. A best-selling second novel about cross-culturalisation by a homegrown author.

Memoirs of Lee Kuan Yew: Vols 1 & 2 by Lee Kuan Yew. Times. Fascinating first-person accounts by Singapore's first Prime Minister, about Singapore's early tumultuous years (Vol 1), and its progress from the third world to the first (Vol 3).

One for the Road and Other Stories: Recollections of Singapore and Malaya by Julian Davison. Topographica. Autobiographical essays about the bygone era of Singapore and Malaysia in the 1950s and 1960s.

Shiok!: Exciting Tropical Asian Flavors by Terry and Christopher Tan. Periplus. A well-presented photographic cookbook, featuring the best of Singaporean cuisine.

Singapore: Architecture of a Global City by Robert Powell *et al.* Archipelago Press. The definitive book of architecture in Singapore; features both public buildings and private houses.

Singapore Women Re-Presented by Chin, Audrey & Constance Singam. Landmark Books. A rich collection of pieces that explore the social issues and conflicts women face in an ever-changing society.

Singapore's 100 Historic Places. Archipelago Press in association with National Heritage Board. An invaluable guide.

Sinister Twilight by Noel Barber. Cassell. Classic account of the fall of Singapore.

INSIGHT
Pocket Guides

Algarve	Cancun &	Hong Kong	Montreal	Seattle
Amsterdam	The Yucatan	Ibiza	Morocco	Seville, Cordoba
Athens	Cape Town	Ireland	Munich	& Granada
Bahamas	Cayman Islands	Ireland's	Nepal	Seychelles
Bali	Chiang Mai	Southwest	New England	Sicily
Bangkok	Chicago	Israel	New York City	Singapore
Barbados	Corfu	Istanbul	New Zealand	Southern Spain
Barcelona	Corsica	Italian Lakes	The Nile	Southwark
Bavaria	Costa Blanca	Jamaica	Oslo and Bergen	Sri Lanka
Bay of Naples	Costa Brava	Kenya	Paris	Stockholm
Beijing	Costa Del Sol	Krakow	Perth	Switzerland
Bermuda	Costa Rica	Kuala Lumpur	Peru	Sydney
Bilbao & Northwest	Crete	Lisbon	Phuket	Tenerife
Spain	Croatia	Loire Valley	Prague	Thailand
Boston	Denmark	London	Provence	Tibet
Brisbane & the	Denver	Los Angeles	Puerto Rico	Tokyo
Gold Coast	Dubai	Madrid	Quebec	Toronto
British Columbia	Dublin	Maldives	Rhodes	Tunisia
Brittany	Fiji Islands	Mallorca	Rome	Tuscany
Bruges	Florence	Malta	Sabah	Venice
Brussels	Florida	Manila	St Petersburg	Vienna
Budapest	Florida Keys	Melbourne	San Diego	Vietnam
Cairns & Great	French Riviera	Mexico City	San Francisco	Washington DC
Barrier Reef	Gran Canaria	Miami	Sardinia	
California, Northern	Hawaii	Milan	Scotland	

ACKNOWLEDGEMENTS

Cover	**VPA**
Backcover	**Jack Hollingsworth/APA**
Photography	**Jack Hollingsworth/APA and**
Pages 69	**Angsana Resorts & Spa**
14	**Archives & Oral History Department**
35	**Asian Civilisations Museum**
81	**Au Jardin Les Amis**
64, 67	**H. Berbar/HBL Network**
26	**Alain Evrard**
68	**Hans Hayden**
16, 37, 38	**David Henley/APA**
6T, 24B, 44, 46T, 77, 84	**David Henley**
12	**Hans Höfer**
7B, 45, 74, 79	**Ingo Jezierski**
29, 32, 49, 80	**Jonathan Koh/APA**
24T	**Bob Krist**
20	**Philip Little**
71	**Kal Muller**
65	**R. Mohd. Noh**
13	**Photobank**
15	**Straits Times Archives**
63	**Morten Strange**
62	**Denise Tackett**
55	**Larry Tackett**
66	**Arthur Teng**
25, 27B	**VPA**
2/3, 34T	**Tony Ying/APA**
54, 70	**Joseph R. Yogerst**
Cartography	**Michael Larby**
Cover Design	**Carlotta Junger**
Production	**Tanvir Virdee/Caroline Low**

© APA Publications GmbH & Co. Verlag KG Singapore Branch, Singapore

INDEX

Register with
HotelClub.com
and get £10!

At **HotelClub.com**, we reward our Members with discounts and free stays in their favourite hotels. As a Member, every booking made by you through **HotelClub.com** will earn you Member Dollars.

When you register, we will credit your account with **£10** which you can use for your next booking! The equivalent of **£10** will be credited in US$ to your Member account (as **HotelClub Member Dollars**). All you need to do is log on to **www.HotelClub.com/pocketguides**. Complete your details, including the Membership Number and Password located on the back of the **HotelClub.com** card.

Over 2.2 million Members already use Member Dollars to pay for all or part of their hotel bookings. Join now and start spending Member Dollars whenever and wherever you want – you are not restricted to specific hotels or dates!

With great savings of up to 60% on over 20,000 hotels across 97 countries, you are sure to find the perfect location for business or pleasure. Happy travels from **HotelClub.com**!

www.insightguides.com

www.insightguides.com

☗ INSIGHT GUIDES

The World Leader in Visual Travel Guides & Maps

As travellers become ever more discriminating, Insight Guides is using the vast experience gained over three-and-a-half decades of guide-book publishing to create an even wider range of titles to serve them. For those who want the big picture, Insight Guides and Insight City Guides provide comprehensive coverage of a destination. Insight Pocket Guides supply personal recommendations for a short stay. Insight Compact Guides are attractively portable. Insight FlexiMaps are both rugged and easy to use. And specialist titles cover shopping, eating out, and museums and galleries. Wherever you're going, our writers and photographers have already been there – more than once.